M000093363

F(X) Leadership Unleashed!

Thomas S. Narofsky

Copyright © 2013 Thomas S. Narofsky

Narofsky Consulting Group, LLC

Papillion, NE

NarofskyConsultingGroup@gmail.com

Cover design by KJ Paperie

All rights reserved

Disclaimer: There is no official endorsement of this book or the material contained herein by the Department of Defense, United States Strategic Command or the United States Air Force. The thoughts, opinions, anecdotes, Inspire or Retire Theorem and the F(X) Leadership concepts are the intellectual property of the Narofsky Consulting Group.

ISBN: 0615804780
ISBN-13: 978-0-615-80478-1

Endorsements

'Thom has utilized his practical experience and advanced degree in leadership to put together a work that will benefit anyone who reads it. He utilizes critical thinking to provide excellent examples and insightful explanations about leadership in action and not just in theory. Some authors simply reiterate old theories that have been tested to death with no solid solutions about what leadership is or should be. Thom's work takes a fresh approach to leadership providing information that is immediately applicable for everyone. Thom's engaging writing style leaps off each page grabbing the reader's attention with plenty of "a-ha" leadership moments!"

Dr. David P. Byers
Assistant Professor (Leadership, Business, and Adult Education)
Bellevue University

"Shared knowledge is power! Throughout the following pages, Thom shares an abundance of knowledge that all leaders need to know and practice to be effective. The models he's incorporated, as well as the stories, are to-the-point and will equip any leader at any level with a solid foundation on which to build a successful organization."

Bob Vásquez, CMSgt, USAF (retired)
Course Director
United States Air Force Academy Center for Character and Leadership Development

"F(X) Leadership Unleashed is a brilliant piece of work on an approach to leadership that will raise a person's performance to a higher standard. This should be part of every leader's tool kit. It is a must read for every inspiring leader who wants to achieve a higher level in leadership. F(X) leadership is a leadership book for emerging, enduring, and experienced leaders!"

Ronald Kriete, CMSgt, USAF (retired)
President Kriete Consulting Group, LLC
Former Command Chief, Air Force Space Command

"As a student of leadership I thoroughly enjoyed the pragmatic approach of this book. It was a great balance of science, art and life experiences of an experienced leader."

Command Sergeant Major James N. Ross
Space and Missile Defense Army Strategic

i

"Thomas Narofsky's, F(X) Leadership, provides a wealth of tried, true, and proven leadership advice which provides clear instruction for aspiring and residing leaders."

Keith W. McIntosh
Vice Chancellor for Information Technology
CIO Pima Community College District

"Thom has succeeded in translating and sharing his lifelong passion onto the pages of this book so others may benefit from his infectious enthusiasm of developing Leaders. A student of leadership for over 30 years, he uses a creative, fun and exciting way to share his inspirational messages, observations and methods with the reader. From his Leadership Insights to the personal vignettes, Thom does a great job of enticing the reader to turn the next page. This is book for anyone who leads people. I'll pull this book off the shelf and refer to it often... it's that good!

Dave Spector, CMSgt, USAF, (retired)
Former Command Chief, Air Mobility Command

"One of most comprehensive leadership books I've read! Thom's F(X) Leadership approach builds on a strong foundation further touching all aspects of what makes a great leader. His style of weaving personal examples along with past and present leaders reinforces the beauty and elegance of the F(X) Leadership model. A "must read" for all Airmen and those who desire to become a great leader!"

Michael A. Babauta, Lt Colonel, USAF (retired)
President, FVT, Inc.

"Thom has done an amazing job of addressing both the Art and Science of Leadership. He provides solid, down to earth examples and an exceptional formula for leadership success. Leaders at any level of an organization would benefit greatly from learning to apply Thom's model."

Evan J. Downey
CEO, Evan J. Downey and Associates, LLC

"F(X) Leadership provides a well thought out book from the perspective of a long and successful military career and from Thom's life experiences, on-going professional studies, and leader observations. I loved the Summary sections of each chapter with the "Key Takeaways" and the "Leadership Applications." What is knowledge without personal application? Here is another great addition to my Leadership Library, that I will no doubt refer to and read again."

Dr. Barry M. Jude, Lead Pastor, New Day Church, Dayton, OH

DEDICATION

This book is dedicated to my wife Dorene and our three sons, Timothy, Joshua and Jacob, our two daughters-in-law, Karis and Rebekah, and to our grandchildren, Titus and Eliza Belle. Thank you for your love and support through the journey.

"If your actions inspire others to dream more, learn more, do more and become more, you are a leader."

John Quincy Adams

CONTENTS

	Acknowledgments	Pg. vi
	Introduction	Pg. 1
	Part One: Personal F(X)	Pg. 7
1	Awaken the Leader Within	Pg. 8
2	The F(X) Leadership Framework	Pg. 16
3	Leadership C2	Pg. 34
4	Leading is Learning	Pg. 49
5	Developing Your Plan	Pg. 61
	Part Two: People F(X)	Pg. 75
6	Inspire or Retire	Pg. 76
7	Know Your People	Pg. 87
	Part Three: Organizational F(X)	Pg. 103
8	Airmen's Time: The Altus Concept	Pg. 105
9	Collaborative Teamwork	Pg. 119
10	Leadership Models	Pg. 131
11	Strategic Communications Plan	Pg. 142
12	Culture Shift	Pg. 151
13	Building Replacements	Pg. 160
14	Results Driven Leadership	Pg. 171
	Conclusion	Pg. 179
	Chapter Review	Pg. 184
	References	Pg. 199

Acknowledgements

Writing a book takes patience and humility. Over the past 20 months I have written and rewritten what I thought was "The Book." However, after several people reviewed it and provided feedback "The Book" became the "First Draft". Since then, and after several rewrites and reviews, I finally published this book. I would like to formerly acknowledge and thank those that reviewed and provided comments for this book.

- General (retired) Kevin P. Chilton, Former Commander United States Strategic Command and NASA Astronaut

- CMSAF (retired) Rodney McKinley, 15th Chief Master Sergeant of the Air Force

- John Whisler, Vice President, Director of Engineering and Construction KS International

- Keith W. McIntosh, Vice Chancellor for Information Technology and CIO Pima Community College District

- Senator Scott Price, Nebraska State Senator 3rd Legislation District and Vice-Chair of the Government, Military, and Veteran's Affairs

- Lieutenant General (retired) Dave Deptula, President at the Deptula Group, LLC and Senior Military Scholar, Center for Character & Leadership Development, United States Air Force Academy

- Chief Master Sergeant (retired) Curtis Brownhill, Former Command Senior Enlisted Leader, United States Central Command

- Chief Master Sergeant (retired) Dave Spector, Vice President, Tanker Support at Seven Q Seven and former, Command Chief, Air Mobility Command

- Chief Master Sergeant (retired) Scott Dearduff, President, Dearduff Consulting LLC and former Command Chief, United Stated Air Forces Central Command

- Terry Narofsky, Director Strategic Procurement at Time Warner Cable

Introduction

I believe that leadership principles are timeless and apply across all spectrums of life. This book is a self-development and leadership development book based on my 28 years in the United States Air Force. The stories and examples are primarily military; however, the leadership principles in the book can be used by anyone seeking to grow and develop themselves into a better leader. I challenge you to read the book and learn about the F(X) principles.

The F(X) Leadership Model is about the effects (F(X)) and outcomes you want to produce in your life. It is about you taking ownership of your growth and development and the actions in your life. The F(X) Leadership name is a compilation of the Inspire or Retire Theorem's function of X or F(x), and the Leadership Based Outcomes/Mindset model effects of F(X) based mindset model.

The Theorem and the models have served me well in my approach to self-development and leadership development.

A key part of the F(X) model is the DELTA symbol. The DELTA symbol means change. Change is a constant in life and leadership. Inside the DELTA is the letters C4, which represents Character, Competence, Courage and Commitment. All change starts from the inside first. C4 is the most explosive part of the function of (x) because it represents who you are deep down inside, your abilities, your strengths and your passion.

Outside the DELTA symbol are the letters CG for Continuous Growth, CD for Continuous Development and CR for Continuously Reinventing yourself. You must be committed to the lifelong journey of developing yourself, your professionalism and your leadership.

Inspire or Retire

The Motto "Inspire or Retire" is a reminder to always inspire yourself and your people. As a leader, if you can no longer inspire your people it is time to step aside and let someone else take the lead. As a leader, you can choose to fan the flames with inspiration or you can extinguish the flames of your people. By being inspiring you can create a team of motivated people and lead your team to succeed.

The Journey

The genesis for this book comes from a leadership development project I had the unique chance to work on called *Airmen's Time*. In the course of the project I implemented, applied and refined my F(X) leadership concepts to grow and develop emerging and enduring leaders.

The journey to write this book started on March 22, 2005. As part of our Airmen's Time leadership development program, I had the opportunity to spend an entire day with Donald T. Phillips, the author of *Lincoln on Leadership*, *The Founding Fathers on Leadership* and other leadership books.

He was invited to Altus Air Force Base to talk about his thoughts on leadership and to be the guest speaker for the Chief Master Sergeant Induction Ceremony. Throughout his visit we discussed the Airmen's Time program, the Leadership Based Outcomes/Mindset model, the F(X) models and my Inspire or Retire Theorem we were using for the development of our emerging and enduring leaders.

At the end of the day, Mr. Phillips pulled me aside and said I needed to document what we were doing and to later publish the results in a paper or in a book. I took his advice to heart and started my journey to writing this book.

In December 2005, I published a preliminary paper titled *Airmen's Time* describing the concepts and models of our development program and the progress so far. In December 2006 I published a follow-on paper titled *Airmen's Time: Building a Leadership-Centered Legacy* describing the impact on the strategic leadership team and the effect of the program on the wing, the Air Force and the Defense Information Systems Agency.

In May 2010, I published my Master's Thesis titled *Airmen's Time: Developing the 21st Century Wingman, Leader, and Warrior* as part of my Masters of Art in Leadership. The thesis synthesized the leadership concepts developed at Altus Air Force Base and my use of them over a five-year period, including my conclusions about personal leadership development. Finally, in December 2010 I started working on the development of this book.

In January 2011, I had the opportunity to dine with Simon Sinek, author of *Start with the Why*, and during dinner he stated, "There are leaders, and there are those who lead. Leaders hold a position of power or authority, but those who lead inspire us."

This provided me a chance to talk to him about my Master's Thesis, the Inspire or Retire Theorem, my F(X) Leadership principles for which I was in the developmental stages of writing my book on personal development and leadership.

He listened as I explained my thoughts. After I was finished talking he said, "You explained the who, what, where and when of your book but not the why. Why are you writing this book? Why is this important to you? And why should other people read the book?" His insightful questions provided me with renewed clarity and purpose for writing this book. Therefore, in the words of Simon Sinek, I will start with the **Why.**

The Why

First, I am passionate about developing emerging, enduring, and experienced leaders and teaching them how to develop themselves using a disciplined and deliberate approach. All leadership begins from inside a person and must be developed and grown as they grow into emerging and enduring leaders.

Second, my next passion is for developing the next generation of leaders who will be the leaders in the military, in government, in business and globally. These are the leaders who will lead in a volatile, uncertain, complex and ambiguous world and must be prepared for leading in chaos.

We will need leaders who can meet and adapt to new challenges, build strategic partnerships, build and sustain human capital organizations, and have the courage to act and react to the challenges.

In addition to these requirements, we need to continue to develop leaders who are flexible, adaptive and are globally and culturally aware. This next generation of leaders must understand how to build and maintain trust, keep their integrity and continue to build their credibility.

Lastly, I believe authentic leaders inspire people to greatness. Inspiration is the ability to breathe life into someone or an organization. Inspiration is a positive influence – a positive reinforcement – we give our people. It ignites desire, ignites creativity and ignites innovation in inspired people.

James MacGregor Burns, in his book, *Leadership*, captures what I believe a leader must do each and every day, "Leadership is leaders acting - as well as caring, inspiring and persuading others to act -- for certain shared goals that represent the values -- the wants and needs, the aspirations and expectations - of themselves and the people they represent."

I have been asked numerous times, "How did you get to have a successful career?" I answer with the same response each time.

HARD WORK!!

Some might describe my career as successful because I had the opportunity to meet, have dinner and spend time with, ambassadors, governors, senators, congressman, defense secretaries, foreign dignitaries, foreign military leadership, CEOs and TV actors.

These opportunities, however, are the result of the hard work and P4R (perseverance, planning, preparation, persistence and resilience) to become an expert and leader in my profession.

Being a successful leader and an expert in your chosen profession requires hard work and P4R. Staying successful as a leader is even harder work! Ask any artist or performer and they will tell you it takes hours of daily practice, and years, to become a master performer or a master artisan.

It takes hours, if not years, of developing, growing, preparing and performing to be a master leader. However, the payoff is worth the hard work. Winston Churchill describes why it is vital that we are prepared and qualified to lead.

> "To every person, there comes in their lifetime that special moment when they are tapped on the shoulder and offered that chance to do a very special thing, unique to them and fitted to their talents. What a tragedy if that moment finds them unprepared and unqualified for the work that would be their finest hour."   Sir Winston Churchill

It is never too early or too late to become a better leader. The process requires continuous growth, continuous development and continuously reinventing yourself on a daily basis. This is also true in life. Leadership, learning and life are synonymous.

How Do I Know That The F(X) Principles Work?

First, I am living proof they work. I applied these principles throughout my life and it has helped me to build a successful professional career, but more importantly, the principles helped me develop and grow myself personally. Second, I had the opportunity to use, share and teach the Inspire and Retire Theorem and F(X) leadership models in an organizational setting in a program called Airmen's Time: The Altus

Concept. Third, I have also shared them in worldwide professional and leadership development seminars with U.S., Korean, Japanese, Kuwaiti, Australian, British, Canadian, Belgian and German enlisted forces. The Theorem and models work if you take the time to apply them to your life.

Bottom Line

Here is the bottom line: If you are looking for an easy fix to becoming a master leader, then this book is not for you. The models and concepts are tools – not a panacea – for the hard work and discipline required to become a master leader.

If, however, you want to be a successful leader in your profession and in life, then this book is a leadership and a life operator's manual to help you succeed.

This book is divided into three parts. Part 1 is about developing your personal leadership using the F(X) Leadership ideas and concepts. It is the Science and Art of F(X) Leadership and individual leadership development.

Part 2 is about developing a People Focused Leadership style using the Inspire or Retire Theorem and the F(X) Model. Leadership is about the people you lead every day. A leader must be passionate about their people and want to develop and grow them.

Part 3 is about Airmen's Time: The Altus Concept, which is about organizational leadership and my first-hand experience on the effects it had on the Air Force. It shows how an organization uses the teach, mentor and coach techniques along with the teaming aspect of growing and developing leaders. It also shows how an organization combines learning and teaching as an organizational tool to develop emerging and enduring leaders.

First, use the book as an informative guide of how to develop yourself and your leadership potential. Second, use the book at the application level and use the theorem, model, leadership lessons and exercises in your own life. Finally, read the book as a story of how you can make a difference in your life and in the lives of your people.

There is nothing more difficult to carry out, nor more doubtful of success, nor more dangerous to handle, than to initiate a new order of things. For the reformer has enemies in all those who profit by the old order, and only lukewarm defenders in all those who would profit by the new order, this lukewarmness arising partly from fear of their adversaries, who have the laws in their favor; and partly from the incredulity of mankind, who do not truly believe in anything new until they have had the actual experience of it."

Niccolo Machiavelli (1469 – 1527)

PART ONE

Personal F(X)

Now is the time to reinvent yourself and develop a new plan of action. Now is the time to create new actions and practices that are focused on growth and development in your personal and professional life. Now is the time to unleash your leadership potential and ignite your passion to lead.

"Nemo dat quod non habet."

You can't give what you don't possess.

Chapter 1

Awaken the Leader Within

> **Key Leadership Concept**: Leadership begins inside of you. Leadership is about you, the people you influence and a belief that you can make a difference and have an impact. Leadership starts with a condition of the heart – the desire and passion to make a difference before it moves to the brain to implement a plan to make a difference. It is an inside-out process and is shaped by your values, character, choices, opportunities, experiences and your worldview.

How do you wake up each morning? Do wake up ready to face the challenges and excited to make an impact or do you meet the morning with a sense of drudgery and despair? Do you have a vision for your life? Do you know where you are going in life? Do you see yourself as limited by your potential or limitless by your opportunities? Are you ready to unleash your leadership and change your life?

If you wake up full of energy everyday focused and ready to live abundantly you probably have identified, and are living your life's purpose and have a vision for your life.

Purpose

Purpose expresses most deeply what makes you a unique individual. Your purpose defines who you are, how you live your life and how you lead. Your purpose provides you with inner strength and drive to live and lead each day. It equips you with what you need to face the challenges of the day and of life. Your purpose provides context and meaning to your life.

Your life and your leadership are driven by one thing...your purpose in life. This is a bold statement to make in the first chapter but I truly believe you are shaped by your purpose in life.

My purpose is the true essence of who I am as a person and how I lead as a leader. My purpose drives me, influences me and shapes my actions and reactions to life. My purpose is not my career or something I do. It is who I am at the center of my core being. My purpose defines my character, my leadership and me. Leadership is not what I do it is who I am. There is no escaping who I am. My leadership is the embodiment of my heart, mind, body and soul. It is an amalgamation of my life's purpose, my values, my ethics, my core beliefs, my life philosophy and my worldview.

My Purpose

My faith in Christ and the military and have helped me to define my purpose. The Air Force Core Values helped to truly shape my life. Integrity First...It is a core value every leader should use. Integrity is leadership authenticity. Excellence in All We Do...Why would you settle for second best in your life? It is about you striving toward your goals and accepting nothing but the very best. Service before Self...a commitment to leading by serving others and a higher purpose.

I served in the Air Force as a Sergeant through Chief Master Sergeant for 24.5 years of my 28 years. The years serving in the capacity of sergeant defined my purpose and shaped my servant leader outlook and leadership competence. To me leading is synonymous with serving.

When you break down the word sergeant it means to serve. The Latin etymology for the word "sergeant" is serviens, meaning "serving." If you use the present active, servio means, "I serve." Therefore, when I retired from the military as Chief Master Sergeant, I retired as a Chief Master Servant. My role was to be a "servant leader who grows the next generation of leaders."

My purpose in life is to serve and develop other people. It is something I have had a passion for throughout the last 28 years. This may sound pedestrian, but it is true. My purpose gave me direction, focus and energy to develop and grow my replacements. My life's purpose defined my life and my career. Even when I retired, my passion for developing my replacements was still a major concern.

End with Purpose

On a hot and muggy day in Nebraska, I was ending my service to our country. I was on the stage with General C. Robert Kehler, General Kevin Chilton, and Command Sergeant Major Pat Alston conducting a Change of Responsibility Ceremony and my retirement from the Air Force after 28.5 years of service. In the audience were family, friends, coworkers and peers, but most of all the enlisted personnel I had the opportunity to serve for the last 3.5 years. I was glad my career was ending in this way.

As I approached the podium to say my closing words to the audience, I reflected on what I was about to say. Here I was getting ready to say goodbye to wearing a uniform and everything I swore to defend for over half my life and all I could think about was my purpose and passion for the last 24 years...developing the next generation of enlisted leaders for service to our country.

"My final comments are really focused on something I am passionate about...Enlisted Force Development. I authored two papers on the subject and spent many years working on this in the Air Force and the Joint Environment. In the 21st century environment, I believe our Nation's Security can be strengthened if we continue to develop an enlisted force that will endure as the backbone of our nation's military and is the envy of other nations. Militarily speaking, we cannot continue to train and develop today's enlisted leaders with yesterday's developmental mindset; if we do, we end up fighting asymmetric warfare with Napoleonic tactics, techniques and procedures.

"Enlisted education, leadership development, and professional growth need to prepare our enlisted leaders for today's fight and the challenges for the future. In addition to the complications of the future, we will need leaders who can meet and adapt to new challenges, who will build strategic enlisted partnerships with coalition nations and who understand that Joint Operations is the way to win our nation's wars. I believe that future education, professional growth and leadership requirements for our enlisted force should be focused on character development. We need to breed into our enlisted force the meaning of our core values and a clear understanding of what Honor, Commitment and Country mean.

"We need to make sure the enlisted force has assured technical competence, the courage to act and react and a solid commitment to serving a higher calling. In addition to these requirements, I think we need to continue to develop a flexible, adaptive and globally and culturally aware enlisted force. Leaders who understand how to build and maintain trust and relationships within their Service and across the Services, need to understand they need to leave a legacy of leaders behind them. They need to build their replacements.

"We need to have an Enlisted Force that understands Servant Leadership, because, in the end it is not about me--never has been, never will be. It is about my Country and the people I serve every day. Well, at last it has arrived, the end of our military service. I thoroughly enjoyed my 28 years in the Air Force. It has been an honor and a pleasure to serve."

If your career ended tomorrow, would you still have a sense of purpose in your life? If the answer is "no," then you do not have a well-defined purpose. Your life's purpose is not defined by your career. Your life's purpose defines your career. Unfortunately, many people live their lives without defining their purpose, or worse yet, thinking that their career defines them. Your career does not define you...your purpose defines you.

Discovering Your Purpose

Self-awareness is understanding and discovering your purpose and is the key to your success as a leader. How do you discover your purpose? Your purpose is a matter of reflecting on who you are, what excites and motivates you and what you feel called to do. Just like you need oxygen to breathe and survive, you need a life's purpose to thrive and survive.

Discovering your life's purpose is a process of self-discovery and self-awareness. Part of self-discovery is defining your core values, your beliefs and worldview. Along with your life's purpose, these are the lenses that you see the world through, handle challenges and approach your leadership decisions. To truly understand your purpose you need to know yourself.

Know Yourself

Nosce Te Ipsum is Latin for "Know Thyself". The saying is attributed to many Greek and Roman philosophers to include Socrates, Aristotle, Heraclitus and Cicero. This theme of understanding yourself is also a key principle many of today's leadership authors point to as the beginning point for all leaders.

Knowing yourself improves your capability to be flexible and adaptive in different situations, allowing you to work with others during challenging and demanding problems more skillfully and diplomatically. It allows you to use the right capabilities at the right time and in the right situational context. Finally, knowing yourself likewise provides you more confidence in developing yourself for the future.

If you desire to lead and influence others, then you need to be cognizant of your actions, principles and beliefs and be aware of how they shape you and influence others. As human beings, we need to understand we are a complex network of values, beliefs, ideas, traits, capabilities, talents and life experiences. This complex network is our character DNA.

Values

My values shaped my purpose. Values are those core beliefs that you hold dear, live your life around and are unchanging. Our core values are shaped by our core belief system. Values are those things that we hold most dear in our lives: Family, faith, freedom, human dignity, respect for others and integrity are just a few examples. These values and beliefs shape our character and shape how we see the world.

Personal values may be aspects of life we think are important to live our lives with, such as integrity, excellence or service. Together these values are the principles that we see our purpose through. Our values drive our behavior and shape our character.

Faith

My belief in Jesus Christ has shaped my purpose. I believe we serve a higher purpose and that are all created equally in God's Eyes. Treating people with the respect, dignity and equally is what we are called to do. A successful leader needs to be a Servant Leader like Christ, have the wisdom of Solomon, use the tenacity and management skills of Nehemiah, and be a Son of Encouragement like Barnabas.

Worldview

Our worldview is how we look at the world through our values, beliefs and purpose. It is our way of making sense of what is going on in the world and how we cope and act in the world. Our worldview is unique to us.

Character

Character is the outward expression of our purpose, values and worldview. Our character comprises our beliefs, motives, values, desires, behaviors and principles that drive and shape our actions as a leader.

In the book, *Ascent of a Leader*, authors Bill Thrall, Bruce Nicholl and Ken McElrath provide what I consider a good working definition of character. "Character—the inner world of motives and values that shapes our action—is the ultimate determiner of the nature of our leadership."

Your character is tested in the crucible of life and is forged through adversity and trials. The character of a leader is important for many reasons. First, without a solid character foundation, the critical link of trust between leaders and followers will not exist. Second, your character provides a true-north compass-heading for your decisions to do what is right and the capability to avoid what is wrong. Your character and leadership are an outward expression of who you are.

Vision

Life and leadership begins with a clear picture for your life and a vision to fulfill your purpose. Everyone needs a vision in order to know where they are going and how they plan to get there. Vision provides the inspiration and is the starting point for accomplishing your purpose. Vision provides direction for your life.

Be bold in defining your life's vision. What do you see yourself doing or becoming over the next 3, 5, 15, 30 years? How do you plan to get there? Do you see yourself as a victor or a victim? How does your vision fulfill your purpose? Your vision for your life will either hold you back or unleash your potential.

A clear vision reduces the uncertainty and ambiguity that you will face in life and provides direction, order and purpose to your life. A clear and bold vision also creates action. It is the impetus for your to achieve your purpose and life's goals. Without a vision you are driving blind in life. Worse yet, without a vision, you'll waste valuable time and energy trying to achieve your purpose. Why? Because everything you end up doing will be an experiment versus intentional.

F(X) leadership is a proactive to life by creating the effects and outcomes not by reacting to life. F(X) leadership means understanding you purpose, envisioning your future, defining your goals, then developing an action plan to creating the effects and outcomes in life. F(X) leadership begins by translating your purpose and vision into a personal mission statement and implemented by well-defined life and leadership goals.

Personal Vision and Mission Statement

As you continue to develop yourself, you need a way to inspire and focus yourself along your journey. A personal vision and mission statement is a tangible method to write your vision, purpose and long term and short term life goals down. This statement is for you to use as a constant reminder of where you are going in life and what is important. It is part of the inside-out look of the F(X) process by examining your life

Your personal vision statement is a strategic or "big picture" view of your life. The first person you need to inspire is yourself. A personal vision statement is a vision of who you want to become. It is about moving from the "as-is" to the "to-be".

It is a critical look at what you want to become, what you want to accomplish, and what kind of future life you desire. Your personal vision should excite and inspire you to act on your vision through your mission statement. Your personal mission statement is what you plan to do to achieve your vision. Writing your mission statement begins by focusing on your values, your life philosophy, your purpose, talents, skills and your guiding principles.

A personal mission statement is not a one-time event, but an evolving process. As you grow and develop as a leader, your mission statement will change. Your mission statement crystallizes your life, career and leadership focus and shapes your growth and development plan.

Summary

The key to understanding how to lead is to know who you are as a person first. What do you believe in? What do you value? What motivates you? An understanding of your personal strengths and weaknesses allows you to make your leadership more effective. Knowing yourself makes you more effective in your organization, with teams and with others.

"Adhere to your purpose and you will soon feel as well as you ever did. On the contrary, if you falter, and give up, you will lose the power of keeping any resolution, and will regret it all your life."
  Abraham Lincoln

Key Takeaways

Dedicate yourself to finding your purpose

Your purpose provides you context and focus for your life.

Your purpose defines who you are

Discover your purpose and live a fulfilling life.

Your life's purpose makes you unique

Living with purpose means your life and leadership are congruent.

Leadership Application

The following are 10 strategies for understanding who you are:

- An authentic leader serves others
- Leading with your purpose and your core values ensures your life and leadership are congruent
- You are responsible for discovering your life's purpose
- Take time to discover who you really are
- Seek to understand yourself before you seek to understand others
- You are unique. There is no one else like you
- Understand how you see the world through your leadership lens
- Understand how your faith and values affect your leadership
- Know yourself…first
- Find your passionate purpose

Leadership Thought Questions

- What gets you out of bed?
- What are the things that motivate and drive you?
- What do you have a passion for?

Reflective Exercise

Take time to discover your purpose. Get away from the "busyness" of the day and your life and carve out some time to critically think and reflect on your life's purpose. Use the questions below to help you discover your purpose. This may take more than one session of reflection to truly define your life's purpose. Take your time. In the next chapter we will define your vision and mission statement.

1. What am I passionate about?
2. What gives me a purpose to live?
3. What excites and ignites me every day to get out of bed?
4. What inspires me to lead every day?
5. What is my life's purpose?

Notes

_____

_____

_____

_____

_____

_____

_____

_____

_____

Chapter 2

The F(X) Leadership Framework

> **Key Leadership Concept**: The F(X) Leadership Model is a proactive, disciplined approach to improving yourself and your leadership. It is the science behind the art. We cannot control every aspect of our lives; we can, however, prepare ourselves to be flexible and adaptive in how we react to our unexpected life and leadership challenges. Since I cannot control an environment that is volatile, uncertain, complex and ambiguous, I can prepare myself for the uncertainty through a disciplined approach.

As the Command Senior Enlisted Leader for United States Strategic Command, I traveled around the world talking about the role of leaders in an organization and the importance of investing in yourself and your leadership development. On many of my travels, I traveled with Command Sergeant Major (CSM) Pat Alston, who at the time was the Command Senior Enlisted Leader for the Defense Threat Reduction Agency and my future successor.

CSM Pat Alston and I were billed as the Teacher and Preacher when we gave our talks. Pat was the Preacher because he provided the art of leadership and I was the Teacher because I provided the science and process. Coaching people in order to develop and grow them into better leaders has been my passion for the last 28 years. That's the reason I wrote this book.

Dare to Live Greatly!

President Teddy Roosevelt spoke these words at the Sorbonne in Paris, France, on April 23, 1910.

"It is not the critic who counts; not the man who points out how the strong man stumbles, or where the doer of deeds could have done them better. The credit belongs to the man who is actually in the arena, whose face is marred by dust and sweat and blood; who strives valiantly; who errs, who comes short again and again, because there is no effort without error and shortcoming; but who does actually strive to do the deeds; who knows great enthusiasms, the great devotions; who spends himself in a worthy cause; who at the best knows in the end the triumph of high achievement, and who at the worst, if he fails, at least fails while daring greatly, so that his place shall never be with those cold and timid souls who neither know victory nor defeat."

What he was talking about was persevering throughout your life. Teddy Roosevelt was an example of self-development. When he was young, he suffered from asthma and childhood sickness that could have left him weak and fragile throughout his life.

He challenged himself daily, developed his mind and body and put himself in situations which required him to grow in order to overcome what life had put upon him.

On January 6, 1919, President Roosevelt died in his sleep, and under his pillow they found a book he was reading. He continued to learn until the moment he died. President Roosevelt wanted more than an average life and he was willing to step into the ring to fight for a better one. He wanted to make an impact and have his life matter!

Why A Disciplined Approach?

Why is a disciplined approach important in leadership development? Today, in the military and in the corporate world, leadership is a personal and an organizational necessity. A disciplined approach to leadership ensures a leader is prepared to lead and the organization has the necessary leadership talent to be globally competitive and prepared for future challenges.

You cannot control an environment that is volatile, uncertain, complex and ambiguous; however, you can prepare yourself for the uncertainty through a disciplined approach. Developing a disciplined plan outlines your self-improvement goals, strategies and outcomes that will help you take advantage of opportunities and be prepared to meet challenges.

A disciplined approach also allows you to prioritize and categorize your goals so you can target which goals will provide you the most benefit first. When you begin a development plan, you need the right mindset and a "must change" attitude in order to shape and mold your talent. You must want to change and reinvent yourself.

Guitar Lessons

In high school I decided I wanted to play the guitar because I wanted to be a part of a local band. Learning to play the guitar was easy; however, I learned that in order to play the guitar and understand scales, chords and on the spot improvisation, it required hard work and hours of practice.

It required me to get serious and develop a learning strategy and a practice schedule. Over time and with a disciplined approach, I learned the guitar and played in several bands. I never reached the level of Eddie Van Halen or other rock guitarists, but I did achieve a level of guitarmanship. Just like an artist who uses a disciplined approach you need to make your leadership development a deliberate and methodical process that moves you from the "as is" state to the "to be" state.

Solid Foundation

In 1996, with my brother-in-law, Glenn, I built an addition to our house in Arizona. Despite the fact I was paying for the construction and acting as the general contractor, the true master craftsman was Glenn. I was Glenn's apprentice during the entire construction project.

Glenn took the time at each phase of the project to explain the purpose and reason why each step was important and what the result would be if we did not build the house in a disciplined way. Each step of building a house depends on first establishing a solid foundation for the house to be built on.

Without a solid and well-constructed foundation, the house would develop cracks and fractures and collapse as the house expanded and contracted. Add to the foundation the stresses of Arizona heat and Mother Nature it would begin to take their toll if the foundation was weak.

The lessons I learned from this experience was that if something is important in your life and you have a passion for it, you need to have a firm foundation of skills, talents and aptitudes to accomplish it. Furthermore, you need a strategy or a framework to develop yourself and a lifelong commitment to growing yourself to achieve the desired outcome. You need to assess your progress to gauge where you are in your development.

For me, the true art of leadership begins with me as a leader by developing, growing and reinventing myself to be the best leader possible for my people and my organization.

Success Is Hard Work!

Over the past thirty years I have integrated training, education and experience into my leadership and my life. By incorporating them into my life, I established my own leadership philosophy and strategy for developing myself. I also incorporated a unique way for remembering and applying this philosophy.

Since I am a kinesthetic learner I have a propensity to think conceptually and then turn my ideas and thoughts into concrete models or mnemonics. However, my mnemonics are not alphabetic, like Every Good Boy Does Fine (EGBDF) for musical scale representation, but mathematical equations and symbols.

30 Years of Leadership Lessons

The F(X) Leadership Development Process represents what I learned over the past 30 years, serving as a supervisor and frontline leader in the military and serving in leadership roles in several non-profit organizations. It was a way of thinking about my development as a leader, the development of my people and the effect on my organization.

In my pursuit to develop myself, I studied both the art and the science of leadership. The concepts, ideas, models and thoughts in this book are the way I developed and trained myself to be a successful leader.

The F(X) Leadership Model is a proactive and disciplined approach to improving my leadership and myself. There are three main models associated with the F(X) Process:

1) The F(X) Leadership Model – The F(X) Leadership Model is a symbolic way of thinking about the inside-out process of developing my leadership skills and life skills first before investing and developing others. All leadership begins from inside you.

2) The Inspire or Retire Theorem – A mathematical mnemonic of my leadership responsibility to the people in my organization. It is a way to remember to always Inspire or Retire!

3) The Leadership Based Outcomes/Mindset Model – The LBO/M five-stage cycle process is from the briefing titled, *Effects-based Operations: Change in the Nature of War*, authored by Lieutenant General David A. Deptula (Retired.), and first published by the Aerospace Education Foundation in 2001.

F(X) Leadership Model

The first model is the F(X) Leadership Model. You are the key to the F(X) model and to your leadership success. The F(X) Leadership Model is a symbolic way of thinking about the inside-out process of developing your leadership skills and life skills first before investing and developing others. The function of (x) is you.

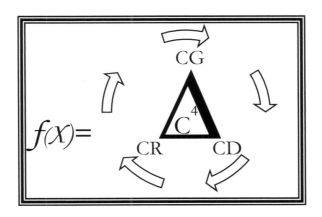

Δ	• The Greek symbol DELTA represents change or difference. Change as a leader is a constant. The changes you make daily and throughout your life will make a difference in your leadership and your life.
C4	• Character, Competence, Courage and Commitment – C4 is the most explosive part of the function of (x) because it represents who you are deep down inside, your abilities, your strengths and your passion.
CD	• Continuous Development – As a leader you must continually develop yourself professionally, technically, mentally, spiritually and physically to stay on the leading edge and to be the example for others to follow.
CG	• Continuous Growth – Growth is the discipline and commitment to apply and incorporate the learned development to your character and leadership abilities.
CR	• Continuously Reinventing Yourself – As you grow and develop your character, your leadership abilities, your competence and your capabilities, you will continually reinvent who you are and what you are capable of accomplishing.

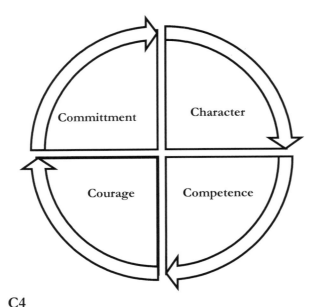

C4

Why is C4 vital to your leadership and to you as a leader? You have control over each of these characteristics in your life. Character, courage and commitment all start from inside, and your competence is an outward growth of you.

It is the most explosive part of the model because it represents whom you are deep down inside, your abilities, your strengths and your passion. These characteristics need to be developed continuously and deliberately. When you improve your C4, you improve and shape your life and your leadership.

Continuous Development

The first way you improve your C4 is through Continuous Development or CD. You must continually develop yourself physically, mentally, spiritually and emotionally to stay on the leading edge and to be the example for others to follow. This type of development hones your life competencies and builds resiliency into your life.

CHARACTER

Integrity is the cornerstone of a leader's character.

It is the stamp of an authentic leader.

Integrity must remain intact or a leader loses credibility and becomes untrustworthy.

COURAGE

Today's leader must display personal and moral courage daily.

Courageous leadership is setting and enforcing the standards daily and being a living example for your people every day

Continuous Growth

The second way is through Continuous Growth or CG. Coupled with your continuous development of your internal and external capabilities and abilities is the continuous growth process. Growth is your self-discipline and self-commitment to apply and incorporate the lessons learned during your development to your character and leadership abilities. Without growth, you will never become the leader you want to be or need to be.

Continuously Reinventing Yourself

Finally, the last part of the model is CR, which stands for Continuously Reinventing Yourself. As you grow and develop your character, competence, leadership abilities and your capabilities, you will continually reinvent who you are and what you are capable of accomplishing. A good way to remember this: as you grow and develop, you are expanding your mind and changing your life.

F(X) Philosophy

In the F(X) process, the successful leader is defined as one who leads oneself first before seeking to lead others. F(X) Leadership is both a philosophy about personal development and leadership development.

It is a set of realistic concepts that people can apply to developing and growing themselves first, then their people and organization.

The F(X) Leadership approach focuses on the leader, the follower and the organization. The personal power of the leader increases the strength of the team and the strength of the organization when the power of F(X) Leadership is unleashed.

F(X) Leadership comes from within the leader and is fueled by the passion and desire to change, to improve and to inspire. Everything you can become and want to achieve comes from the fire within you. You are the key to your success and it begins with a P4R mindset.

COMPETENCE

Properly developed and well qualified in each area of growth and development.

Ability to act and react with the right action at the right time.

COMMITMENT

An unwavering choice to grow and develop yourself on a daily basis.

An unyielding choice to be responsible and accountable for your life and your choices.

Power of a P4R Mindset

P4R (planning, preparation, persistence, perseverance and resilience) is another key part of the F(X) philosophy and leadership model. Being the best in your life, career or leadership requires a P4R mindset.

Planning

Planning is the process of developing actions or plans to attain your desired goals or outcomes for your life or leadership. When making your plans consider what you truly want to accomplish and what effects are needed to achieve your outcome.

Preparation

Preparation is process of equipping and focusing yourself on achieving your plan. You must have the right mindset and focus to carry out your plan successfully. Roman philosopher Seneca said that "Luck is what happens when preparation meets opportunity." Make yourself lucky by being prepared.

Persistence

The objective of persistence is to achieve a goal or outcome in your life. Persistence allows you to keep working at your goal or outcome it until we reach the desired outcome. It is pressing on towards the goal despite all odds. Persistence permits us to attain victory when others have long abandoned the journey.

Perseverance

Perseverance is to endure a difficult situation with resolute determination and to stay in a situation even when we would rather give up even though it is difficult. John Quincy Adams said, "Courage and perseverance have a magical talisman, before which difficulties disappear and obstacles vanish into air."

Perseverance requires our entire emotional, physical, and spiritual forte to tolerate or overcome the situation. By persevering and not giving in you gain strength in your life and leadership.

Resilience

Resiliency is keeping strong emotionally, physically, mentally, and spiritually to be fit, healthy, positive, and prepared for all life's challenges. When you have a firm understanding of your life's purpose, you are more resilient to adversity.

You must make your mind up from the very beginning of the journey to plan and prepare for the journey. Know where you want to go, then plan and chart out the journey. The road to building yourself is demanding, so prepare yourself mentally, physically, spiritually and emotionally for the journey.

Green Bay Packers Coach Vince Lombardi said that success is being your very best.--"The price of success is hard work, dedication to the job at hand, and the determination that whether we win or lose, we have applied the best of ourselves to the task at hand."

Three Core Competencies

There are three competency areas that I develop and grow on a continuous basis. These three areas of growth and develop are a whole person concept. As you grow and develop these areas, you stay balanced and quickly recognize that all three areas define who you are. No one area defines you. You are the sum of all three parts.

Personal

Personal Competency is the C4 of your life. This area has been developing since you were born but never stops growing and developing. This competency is the most important to develop and grow because it is the foundation of your professional and leadership competence areas.

Professional

Professional Competency is your career or professional pursuit. It does not define you as a person but it is the area of your learned expertise. It is a vital part of you as it helps you meet areas in Maslow's Hierarchy of Needs Model.

Leadership

Leadership Competency is your leadership ability and capability. This competency is both your self-leadership and your team and organizational leadership. You must continue to develop this area of expertise as you grow your professional expertise.

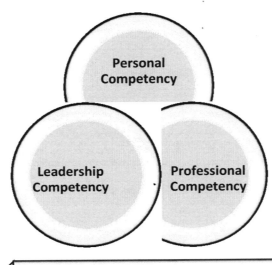

Personal Competency	• You the Person -- Values, Purpose, Character, Worldview, Communication, Relationships, Respect, Dignity, Integrity and Trust, Lifelong Learner and Resiliency
Professional Competency	• You in Your Career -- Technical Skills, Talents, Aptitudes, Education, Training, Experience, Management Skills, Results and Outcome Driven, Lead Change and Critical Thinker
Leadership Competency	• You as a Leader -- Leadership Skills, Talents, Aptitudes, Development, Leadership Opportunities, Experience, Alliances, Authenticity, Visionary, Service Attitude, Creative Thinker, Talent Developer and Culture Creator

While living in Germany I hosted a leadership and professional development seminar focused on the personal, technical and leadership competencies. The guest speakers for the leadership panel were three CEOs from U.S. firms operating in Germany.

The CEO panel was asked which of the three competencies were the most important and why. The CEO, Dave Warner, who operated an IT firm, addressed the forum and said "Personal competency is the most important of the three. You cannot lead if you are personally incompetent. If you don't understand who you are, how you operate, what your leadership blind spots are and how to overcome them, then you cannot lead others effectively." His statement that you are personally incompetent if you cannot lead yourself made an impact on the audience.

Create a Masterpiece

Envision yourself sitting at an old potter's wheel with a lump of clay on the wheel head. You begin to work the foot pedal, the wheel turns and the clay rotates. Your hands surround the clay and you start to apply pressure to even the clay out and to force it to take form.

As you work the core of the clay, you start to form a hole. With each new turn of the wheel, the hole widens and the walls of the clay start to take shape. You continue to turn the wheel, you begin to add water to the clay as you turn and the vessel starts to become smooth and look finished.

With the final turn of the wheel, the shape of the vessel begins to be revealed and the true art is recognized. The true art is your life. Your purpose, values and worldview guides your hand as the clay rotates around the wheel and molds and shapes your life. Just as the master artisan creates a masterpiece with the clay, you are creating a masterpiece as you grow and develop yourself.

The Three Stages of a Leader

A leader grows in the same method a tree grows. A tree grows in three ways throughout its life.

- Roots which tunnel into the ground and establish a solid foundation for the tree

- Shoot tip, which grows upward to increase the height of the tree

- Tree diameter to support the upward growth of the tree and to expand the boundary of the trees territory

The Emerging Leader

The seed of leadership begins to grow and the foundation of their leadership begins to take root in their lives. Emerging leaders need time to build their personal, professional and leadership core competencies to establish rings of growth and development. They seek out opportunities for experience in order to harden their core skills.

The Enduring Leader

The growth rings of leadership start to grow and expand the boundary of the leader. An enduring leader continues to build a solid foundation in their personal, professional and leadership core competence to ensure they are well rooted in their skills. They have experienced success and failures as a leader and have learned valuable lessons that they can use as a leader. An enduring leader continues to seek out opportunities for growth and development and opportunities to use their skills to sharpen their capability.

The Experienced Leader

The signs of growth and develop are present and the maturity of the leader is evident. The experienced leader's years of growth, development, experience and life lessons have produced a harden core of personal, professional and leadership skills and critical thinking. The experienced leader now is a developer of other leaders and takes the time to invest their talents and skills into emerging and enduring leaders.

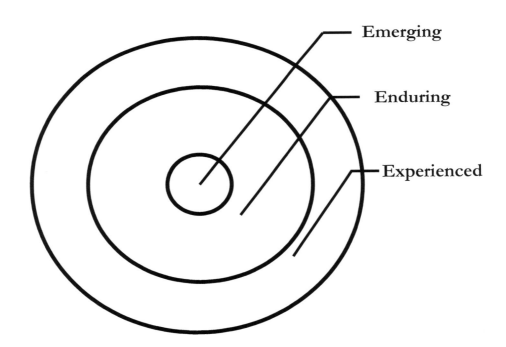

Three Levels of Leadership

There are three levels of leadership—Tactical, Operational and Strategic

Tactical

The tactical level is the first form of leadership. It is learning to lead yourself first. Learning to lead and manage your life is the critical first step in leadership. You must be able to control and regulate yourself in order to lead others.

Operational

The operational level is leading teams or leading others. It is the next level of leadership and is about leading others to accomplish the organizational mission. Operational leadership has the ability to influence the growth and development of two or more people and is a critical leadership role in any organization.

Strategic

The strategic level is leading in an organization. The last stage of leadership is leading in an organization or leading the organization. Strategic leadership spans across many teams, divisions or directorates and has the ability to influence a multitude of people.

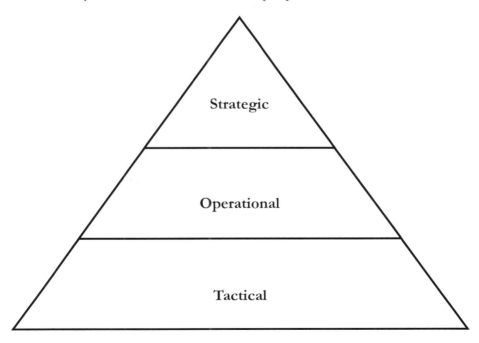

Summary

The F(X) Leadership Model is a disciplined approach and a proactive process that can help you improve yourself and your leadership. Nevertheless, you need to be willing to put in the hard work and dedication to developing, growing and reinventing yourself. Understanding the approaches, models, and concepts is the first key to understanding the F(X) Leadership Process and will help to define your personal vision and mission statement.

The clearer your life's goals are the more likely you will achieve them. Taking the time to sit and define your purpose, your vision and goals will help you to chart your course to achievement. Reflect on what you learned in the first two chapters to establish your personal vision and mission statement. This understanding will lead you to define your leadership growth and development plan.

A leadership growth and development plan is a roadmap of where you, as a leader, want to go in your career and in life. A growth and development plan allows you to express your vision for your life and your leadership, to define your specific goals and objectives and to commit yourself to continuous development and continuous growth actions.

Notes

_____

_____

_____

_____

_____

_____

_____

_____

Key Takeaways

Dedicate yourself to a disciplined approach to life

You cannot control every aspect of your life; however, you can prepare yourself through a disciplined approach to your leadership and your life.

Being successful requires hard work and P4R

Become the master artisan, performer or leader you want to be – develop and grow yourself.

Leadership is an art and a science

If you want to be an effective leader, know both parts of leadership.

Leadership Application

The following are 10 strategies for becoming an F(X) leader:

- You are responsible for your growth and development

- Develop and grow yourself daily

- Seek to achieve mastery of your life and leadership to lead and dare greatly

- Leadership is a performance art so create a masterpiece out of your life

- Perseverance, planning, preparation, persistence and resilience are keys to your growth and development

- Give yourself the time to discover your life's passion

- Clarify your leadership strategy and life vision

- Seek to continuously reinvent yourself

- Seek to continuously grow yourself

- Seek to continuously develop yourself

Leadership Thought Questions

- What is your leadership development strategy?

- What leadership books are you reading?

- What leadership training/seminars have you attended?

F(X) Insight

- **Take your development seriously**

- **Understand how to develop yourself in a disciplined and methodical way**

- **Learn from your successes and setbacks**

- **Execute, then continually evaluate your plan**

- **Make adjustments to your plan to achieve your goals**

Insightful Exercise

The purpose of this writing exercise is to write your personal vision and mission statement. On a separate piece of paper or in the notes section below, write down your core values, what you believe in, what you value most in your life (family, faith, community, etc.); what you want to accomplish in your life and the legacy you want to leave. This exercise, or life record, will highlight what your mission or life's purpose is.

Notes

_____

_____

_____

_____

_____

_____

_____

_____

_____

_____

_____

_____

F(X) Leadership Growth and Development Plan

After reading this chapter, review and reflect on the ideas and concepts presented. Think about how to integrate the ideas or concepts into one of the three growth and development areas--Personal, Professional or Leadership Competency. Think about what opportunities, challenges, resources or blind spots you may encounter when you begin your growth and development journey. Use the following questions to help you grow and develop.

1. What area will the ideas and concepts help me grow and develop?

   - Personal

   - Professional

   - Leadership

2. How will I incorporate this new talent or skill into my development?

3. What is my timeline for learning the new talent or skill?

4. What opportunity and resources exist for me to use this new talent or skill?

   - _____

   - _____

   - _____

5. What blind spots may derail me from using this new talent or skill?

   - _____

   - _____

   - _____

Chapter 3

Learning is Leading!

Key Leadership Concept: A commitment to a lifelong process of learning is the key to successful leadership. In today's volatile, uncertain, complex and ambiguous environment, learning is vital to your ability to adapt to ever-evolving challenges and uncertainty. Continuous learning, continuous development and continuous growth create the self-awareness for a leader to continually reinvent their capability as a leader and a person.

I first met Brian in 1997 when I arrived in Germany. At that time, he was an information infrastructure technician and was satisfied with his life. In his mind, he had achieved everything he set out to since high school. He was the resident expert and the go-to person to fix any problem. Everybody knew him and sought his advice.

A Lifelong Learner

However, although he was satisfied, he was not happy and had begun to look for new opportunities and challenges in his career and life. He felt he needed something more than just being the expert – he wanted to be a leader, too.

After a brief time of mentoring and coaching Brian, he established a growth and development plan of lifelong learning to help in his leadership development pursuit. Brian enrolled in college and stepped up for several leadership opportunities in the organization to learn more about being a leader. I left after a year in the organization but kept track of Brian and his development.

> "Leadership and learning are indispensable to each other."
>
> John F. Kennedy

Brian continued to pursue educational opportunities and leadership roles to increase his leadership capacity and capability. After 16 years of growth and development and several promotions, Brian was promoted to run the organization's Talent Management Directorate. Today, he oversees resident and non-resident education and training courses to increase the professional and personal development of the organization's global workforce. The key to his success was that he improved himself daily and had a clear understanding of his capabilities and abilities as an individual.

Ship Captain

If you watch the television reality show *Deadliest Catch*, then you know that the mission of each ship is to catch crab and make money in the shortest amount of time. Filling the boat and catching your quota quickly means a higher return for the boat and for the crew.

However, you will notice right away each ship is run differently because each Captain is different. The Captain is the leader and sets the organizational culture and code of conduct for the organization. The attitude of the crew and the culture on the boat are a reflection of the Captain's attitude and the code of conduct he articulates.

For ships with one leader this culture and conduct does not change. However, for those boats with two leaders, like the Northwestern and the Time Bandit, the attitude and culture changes as each leader changes. It is interesting to watch the dynamic of the crew and the leader during this changeover. Traditionally, each leader runs his ship based on how he was raised up by his father in the fishing fleet, his experience as a deck hand, his values and his education.

Each Captain is a product of lifelong learning. Through continuous training, education and experience each leader develops and grows from the junior employee to the senior leader.

Develop and Grow Yourself

One of the best lessons I learned early in my career was to have a plan for lifelong learning in order to develop and grow myself. If I wanted the opportunity to be a good leader and a good supervisor, I needed to improve myself. My success is a by-product of lifelong learning. Throughout my career I learned about my capabilities, my values, my potential and myself. I learned how to follow, then learned how to lead and finally learned how to serve.

My early leadership skills were immature and I needed time to develop my people and communication skills. As soon as I could I enrolled in leadership and management courses in college and talked to my supervisor and other leaders in my organization to find out what I needed to learn to become a better equipped leader.

Leadership requires a commitment to enduring learning. A leader knows and understands their strengths, weaknesses, capabilities, abilities and their emotions. A leader needs self-insight into how they operate, how they make decisions and how to treat people in order to lead people.

In order to get ahead in your work, in your life or as a leader, you need to commit to deliberate and continuous learning. This is an indispensable element of leadership. As a leader you need to ask yourself-- What do I need to learn today to be a better leader? What leadership skills or management techniques will help me be more effective? What are my blind spots that I need to fix?

As a learning leader, you need to read leadership books, attend leadership workshops and seminars, look for opportunities for leadership challenges at work and go out into your community and look for leadership opportunities. These are ways to improve your leadership skills and apply what you learned in leader roles. These are the principles of continuous development, growth and reinventing yourself.

> **"No one is free who has not obtained the empire of himself. No man is free who cannot command himself."**
>
> **Pythagoras**

Be a Know it All

Leaders as learners are vital to learning organizations. Today, the workplace is dependent on knowledge capital. As a leader you need to keep that knowledge base in the organization and on your team. You can do that by building the relationship you have with your subordinates each day. A key to your success is to be a know it all leader. Successful leadership requires that you know yourself, know you your people and know your organization.

First, Know Yourself

Learn about your skills and capabilities and take control of your life and leadership. A leader knows and understands their strengths, weaknesses, capabilities, abilities and their emotions. This is the key to becoming a better leader. "Knowing yourself and being reflective about your own behavior is essential to realizing your potential and having positive relationships with others" (Denhardt, Denhardt, and Aristigueta, 2009, p. 17).

Second, Know Your People

Leadership requires you know your people and continue to build the relationship you have with your subordinates or followers. You need to be a leader who influences and inspires others and helps them grow and develop. Positive teamwork supports the organization's goals and objectives, and fosters behavior directed toward the achievement of those ends. Teamwork that supports hard work, loyalty, quality consciousness or concern for customer satisfaction is an example of positive team norms.

Third, Know Your Organization

Grow and develop yourself and your people to make your organization better. A successful leader knows the goals, objectives, priorities, vision and mission of the organization. A leader is dedicated to accomplishing the mission and strives toward mission success.

Enduring Learning Cycle

In a global society that prizes knowledge more than manufacturing, a knowledge-enabled worker is a critical asset to a globally competitive organization. Knowledge is the new capital for an organization.

Knowledge-enabled leaders in an organization provide the necessary competitive edge needed to strive in the global marketplace. Lifelong learning is the way to meet the requirement for the individual and an organizational. One model I developed – similar to the F(X) Leadership Model – is the Enduring Learning Cycle. It is a constant reminder that learning is a lifelong process and necessary to be a better leader every day. The model demonstrates learning is not a one-time event, but a continuous process of continuous development (CD), continuous growth (CG) and continuous experience (CE) that you internalize to shape your Character, Competence, Courage and Commitment (C4). Not only are education and learning an individual and organizational imperative, I believe they are the key to life's success.

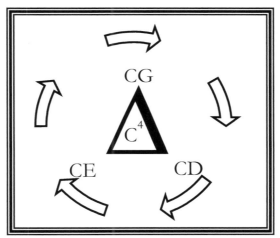

- • The Greek symbol DELTA represents change or difference. Change as a leader is a constant. The changes you make daily and throughout your life make a difference in your leadership and your life.

  Δ

- • Character, Competence, Courage and Commitment – C4 is the most explosive part of the function of (x) because it represents who you are deep down inside, your abilities, your strengths and your passion.

  C4

- • Continuous Development – As a leader you must continually develop yourself professionally, technically, mentally, spiritually and physically to stay on the leading edge and to be the example for others to follow.

  CD

- • Continuous Growth – Growth is the discipline and commitment to apply and incorporate the learned development to your character and leadership abilities.

  CG

- • Continuous Experience – The lifelong model adds your life and leadership experiences to the continuum. Experience is the lesson we learn as a leader that we need to apply to our growth and development.

  CE

10 Reasons for Enduring Learning

- Enduring learning allows you to identify your strengths and weaknesses to improve your leadership effectiveness.

- Enduring learning helps you become more self-aware and improves your leadership capability.

- Enduring learning increases your potential in your personal life, your organization and with your people.

- Enduring learning will improve your decision-making and thinking skills in your life and leadership.

- Enduring learning will help you be more flexible and adaptive in your personal and professional life.

- Enduring learning keeps you in the driver's seat and keeps you more in control of your future.

- Enduring learning helps you stay competitive by developing new capabilities and skills.

- Enduring learning increases your capability for critical thinking and logical analysis.

- Enduring learning provides an opportunity to take responsibility for your life, actions, behaviors and decisions.

- Enduring learning allows you to take risks and move beyond your secure comfort zones.

Self-Leadership

To be a great leader you need to understand who you are and how you operate as a human being first before you can lead others. This is self-leadership. Self-leadership requires a commitment to lifelong learning. A leader knows and understands their strengths, weaknesses, capabilities, abilities and their emotions. An engaged leader needs self-insight into how they operate, how they make decisions and how to treat people, in order to lead people.

Grow and Develop

These are some ways to improve your leadership skills and apply what you have learned in leader roles. These are the principles of continuous growth, development and reinventing yourself.

Read

Become a reading sponge and soak in knowledge. Read books, articles and critical reviews in your technical expertise to improve and develop your professional competence. At the same time, read books and articles concerning leadership and self-development to build and grow yourself and your leadership competency.

Workshops and Seminars

Attend workshops and seminars to stay current on up-to-date information concerning your career and leadership. Use workshops and seminars to fill in gaps in your learning and to learn new techniques, tactics and procedures.

Educational Opportunities

Seek out educational opportunities to grow yourself. Use college and continuing education courses to grow and develop your critical thinking skills and your breadth of knowledge.

> Experience: that most brutal of teachers. But you learn, my God do you learn.
> **C.S. LEWIS**

Experience

An important part of the developmental process is leadership and life experiences. Experience is a valuable teacher and a necessary part of leadership growth. A major challenge early in your career can shape how you react and deal with future leadership challenges.

Today's effective leaders had opportunities early in their careers requiring them to lead, take risks and learn and grow from their successes and failures. Experience is a principal coach, but experience alone does not guarantee development.

Personality and Leadership Assessments

Throughout my years of leadership I have had the opportunity to use assessment tools to help find out more about who I am as a leader. I used three 360-Degree multi-rater assessments and eleven other assessment instruments to help me further my leadership capability. Through each of these assessments I learned a little more about how I operate as a leader, how I approach decision-making and how I deal relationally with other people.

Leadership Opportunities

Seek out opportunities to lead in your organization, in your community or in a non-profit organization. The ability to use and exercise your leadership skills will help you to grow as a leader and help you develop your decision-making skills. Leadership opportunities will also stretch you.

Teach, Coach, Mentor

The best way to learn, grow and develop yourself is to turn around and teach, coach and mentor others. Teaching a skill or talent ensures that you ingrain the skill or talent into your life. By teaching, you learn twice.

I have had the opportunity to follow in the tracks of some great leaders and not-so-great leaders. I have learned from them all. The not-so-great leaders taught me how to be a better leader by not following their example and learning from their lack of leadership. However, it is the examples and mentoring of the great leaders that honed and forged me into the leader I am today.

Several key enlisted leaders along the way who increased my leadership capability and ability: Chief Master Sergeant (CMSgt) Ron Kriete; CMSgt Tim Carroll; CMSgt Darryl Leach; CMSgt Todd Small; CMSgt Ken McQuiston; CMSgt Timmothy Dickens; CMSgt Rob Tappana; CMSgt Scott Dearduff; CMSgt Dave Spector; Force Master Chief Chuck Dassance; Command Sergeant Major Jeff Mellinger; Fleet Master Chief "Lump" Nissen; Fleet Master Chief Roy Maddocks; Command Sergeant Major Mike Balch; CMSAF Gerald Murray; CMSAF Rod McKinley; CMSAF James Roy; Senior Enlisted Advisor to the Czechoslovakian Ministry of Defense, Command Sergeant Major Ludek Kolesa; and the Senior Enlisted Advisor to the Chairman, Joint Chiefs of Staff, Sergeant Major Bryan Battaglia.

Several key Officers in my career increased my leadership opportunities and provided me with the latitude to operate: Lt Colonel Mike Baubauta; Colonel Rob Borja; Colonel Paul Curlett; Brigadier General Dave Warner; Brigadier General Patrick Higby; Brigadier General Steven Spano; Major General Mark Solo; Major General Carlton Everhart; Major General Mark Dillon; Major General Abe Turner; Lieutenant General Carroll Pollett; Vice Admiral Van Mauney; General William Shelton; General Kevin Chilton; and General C. Robert Kehler.

Leadership Awareness

Emotional Intelligence

Stress, emotions and moods are key reasons why I think emotional intelligence is an important leadership necessity. Each leader is susceptible to his or her emotional state and moods at work. Understanding how to manage your emotions and moods can make you a better leader.

According to Daniel Goleman in his book *Emotional Intelligence*, self-awareness, self-management, social awareness and relationship management are vital assets for a leader. An emotionally intelligent leader understands that emotions can help or hinder their leadership abilities.

Decision-making

Your choices determine who and what you are and can become. C.S Lewis, English professor and author of *The Chronicles of Narnia*, stated, "Every time you make a choice, you are turning the central part you – the part that chooses – into something little different than what it was before. Taking your life as a whole, with innumerable choices, you are slowly turning this thing into a heavenly creature or a hellish creature."

All of us are living with the decisions we made yesterday, last year and years gone by. The choices we made determined who we are, what we are and where we are today. Many of us made choices without a clear understanding of the kinetic impact the 2nd, 3rd or 4th order-of-effect of that decision would have on our futures.

Decisions Have Consequences

The one thing I have learned during my leadership journey is that a leadership failure can be a leadership success. To put this in perspective, failing is not the end of your role as a leader, most times, it is the beginning of a leadership learning cycle. As a leader, I do not fear failure as much as I fear succeeding at trivial or unimportant things in life.

Failure can be a very good life lesson as well as a leadership lesson as long as you learn from it and do not give up because of the setback. My best leadership lessons have been through trial and error and failing. My success as a leader has been built on not letting my failures define me or keep me from leading.

One defining leadership setback for me was when I was fired from the United States Air Forces in Europe Computer Systems Squadron while I was serving as the Superintendent of the Information Assurance Branch.

In 1998, I was leading a team of six information assurance professionals and we were developing the communications security operations plan for all inbound aircrews deploying into the European airspace for Operation Allied Force and Operation Shining Hope.

As air operations grew, our team grew from 6 to 12 persons and our communications security operations grew too. We acquired six tons of North Atlantic Treaty Organization and Joint Staff codebooks and keying material for the day-to-day air operations.

Throughout Operation Allied Force, we trained 200 aircrews, directed 22 courier missions to 8 countries for material delivery and had 100 percent accountability of all classified material. The communications security operations plan was a success and we met every objective assigned.

The team won high praise from the Director of Communications and Information Systems, Brigadier General Michael Peterson and from the Commander, United States Air Forces in Europe, General John P. Jumper for successful execution of our plan and for ensuring day-to-day air operations had the correct material and books. As a leader, I was very proud of my team.

The day after air operations ceased I was dismissed from my position. The reason cited was failure to communicate with my direct leadership. First, my direct leadership was correct, I failed to inform them on what we were doing in executing the plan. It was a conscious leadership decision that I took based on my previous experience as the communications security officer for the 612th Air Operations Center.

Although I made the mission happen, I failed to communicate correctly the necessity for expedience to my direct leadership.

Second, I chose after the dismissal to communicate better with my next leaders. When I arrived at the 786th Communications Squadron, I had the fortunate opportunity to have Captain Robert Borja (now Colonel Borja) and Chief Master Sergeant Darryl Leach as my next leaders. Both of these leaders provided me an opportunity to increase my leadership ability and challenged me to persevere.

Captain Borja provided me with a briefing that Lieutenant General (Retired) Harry Raduege gave as a presentation to the Advanced Communications Officer Class in August 2000 called "Raduege's Formula for Success". This presentation gave me a lot to think about and was the inspiration for the Inspire or Retire Leadership Theorem.

Chief Darryl Leach was a master teacher, mentor, leader and a man of God. He mentored, shaped and molded men and women of the 786th

Communications Squadron, Information Systems Flight. He made us better than when we arrived. Under his leadership he produced award-winning leaders, award-winning organizations and produced ten Chief Master Sergeants from our flight. He made me a better leader, writer and developer of leaders.

Summary

Continuous learning and continuous development creates the self-knowledge for a leader to continually reinvent their capability as a leader and a person. In addition, continuous learning provides a leader the necessary knowledge to stay current on today's trends, but also flexible and adaptive to face tomorrow's challenges.

Leaders see beyond the current problems and limitations to help others see their own possibilities. It is a key part of growth and development. We continue to grow when we help others grow and develop. We develop ourselves while we are developing others. The cycle of growth and development is continuous as long as you continue to develop your skills and integrate your experiences.

I can truly say that I am where I am today because of great teamwork, great mentoring and great opportunity. I have been a part of many teams and I have led many teams in the Air Force. My success has been a by-product of how I learned to follow, then learned to lead and then finally learned how to serve. The one takeaway that I learned from all these leaders is that as a leader you have an opportunity to make an impact on your organization and your people.

Notes

_____

_____

_____

_____

_____

_____

_____

Key Takeaways

Dedicate yourself to lifelong learning

Self-leadership is the key to leading yourself well and then leading others. Be the leader you want to be by developing yourself first.

Read, read and read some more

Reading is a valuable leadership skill for developing yourself. Reading provides new ideas, concepts and opens your mind to further learning. Read biographies of leaders, read leadership books and read books about your profession.

Continue to develop your character

Character development is vital to leadership. Our character is the true essence of who we are as a person and how we lead as a leader. It is the very core of what drives us and influences our actions and reactions. Character defines our authentic leadership.

Leadership Application

The following are 10 strategies for becoming a lifelong learner

- Endeavor to become a lifelong learner in all aspects of your life
- Apply self-leadership practices to create the outcomes you desire
- Understand who you are and what you can accomplish
- Learn from everyone you meet
- Create time to read and grow
- Invest in your growth and development first
- Use your experiences as life and leadership lessons
- Keep your mind open to new ways of thinking
- Apply your growth, development and experiences to your leadership
- Use self-assessments and leadership assessments to find your blind spots and areas needing improvement

Leadership Thought Questions

- What are you doing to grow and develop your leadership skills?
- What leadership books are you reading?
- What leadership training/seminars have you attended?
- How are you teaching your people about leadership?
- How are you developing your character?
- What did you learn in this chapter?
- What significant ideas or points stand out in your mind?

F(X) Insight

- **Leadership is a lifelong process**
- **Learning is a Journey**
- **Leaders must be Learners**
- **Grow and learn everyday**
- **Know Yourself**
- **Seek out opportunities to lead**
- **Use your experiences as a learning tool**
- **Prepare yourself to lead in a VUCA environment**
- **Develop your character, competence, commitment and courage daily**

Reflective Exercise

The purpose of this writing exercise is to review and assess who you really are. On a separate piece of paper or on the lines below, write down the major turning points in your life and your leadership. What are the major events and noteworthy experiences that shaped your life? This exercise, or life record, will highlight events that helped you make decisions, set goals or realize something about yourself. Focus your writing on both negative and positive experiences and what you discovered and learned from them.

Notes

_____

_____

_____

_____

_____

_____

_____

_____

_____

_____

_____

F(X) Leadership Growth and Development Plan

After reading this chapter, review and reflect on the ideas and concepts presented. Think about how to integrate the ideas or concepts into one of the three growth and development areas--Personal, Professional or Leadership Competency. Think about what opportunities, challenges, resources or blind spots you may encounter when you begin your growth and development journey. Use the following questions to help you grow and develop.

1. What area will the ideas and concepts help me grow and develop?

    - Personal

    - Professional

    - Leadership

2. How will I incorporate this new talent or skill into my development?

3. What is my timeline for learning the new talent or skill?

4. What opportunity and resources exist for me to use this new talent or skill?

    - _____

    - _____

    - _____

5. What blind spots may derail me from using this new talent or skill?

    - _____

    - _____

    - _____

Chapter 4

Leadership C2

> **Key Leadership Concept**: Characteristics are leadership attributes, qualities or unique aptitudes and leadership competencies are behaviors, skills or talents for a specific profession or responsibility. In order to develop your leadership growth and development plan you need to identify the leadership characteristics and competencies that will improve your capability and prepare you for future opportunities. Your developmental plan should incorporate skills training, leadership experiences, growth opportunities and leadership knowledge development.

The world has changed; it is a volatile, uncertain, complex and ambiguous environment. The overarching theme in the collected data in both the military and in the corporate world is a call to develop and prepare leaders to operate in a world of globalization, global diasporas, global markets, social media, technological advances and the unyielding pace of change in both the military and business operations.

No Passengers or Bystanders

From August 2006 to July 2007 I deployed in support of Operation Iraqi Freedom. During my deployment, I traveled to see our Airmen and to participate in their combat missions. One of the missions the Airmen conducted was to dominate the battle space surrounding Forward Operating Base Bucca through integrated base defense and aggressively securing multiple convoy routes utilizing mounted and dismounted combat patrols within a 300 square kilometer Area of Influence.

The battle space they operated in had 20 Improvised Explosive Device attacks on patrols resulting in the loss of lives. Over the course of my deployed time, I conducted multiple mounted combat patrols and dismounted combat patrols "outside the wire" searching for improvised explosive devices, standoff threat positions and insurgent activity with these Airmen.

There are two ways to travel to Bucca – by air on Blackhawk Helicopters or by land via a combat convoy. Both can be dangerous. Throughout the year, I convoyed many times on cross-border convoys through the dangerous roads of Iraq.

No matter if I headed out via a combat convoy or out to conduct a mounted or a dismounted combat patrol, the Troop Commander briefed me on what my role and responsibility was during the patrol.

The most important part of the briefing was: there are no passengers or bystanders on a combat convoy or combat patrol. You are a combat-trained leader ready to engage and suppress the enemy if so challenged.

Today, there is no room for leaders who want to be passengers or bystanders in leadership. The reality is the world changed; it is a volatile, uncertain, complex and ambiguous environment.

VUCA or the New Normal

In 1994, futurist John Peterson, in his book *Road to 2015*, stated that the period of time we are living today is in constant change and flux and the rate and change is greater than any time in history. In his book he indicates that change will only increase as time goes and fundamentally change how we live our lives.

In 1996, Peter Vaill published his book, *Learning as a Way of Being: Strategies for survival in a World of Permanent White Water*, described the rate and complexity of change for organizations as "permanent white water." The rate and pace of change is constantly producing upheaval and churn in our lives.

Along with this new call we also have a new environment to contend with and will continue to challenge and shape these new leaders. Psychologist

VUCA

Volatile

means that the speed, size, scale of change in the world today has a great impact on events around the globe almost instantaneously.

An example is the rate and pace of stock market changes and the effect it has on personal and corporate wealth.

Uncertainty

means that world events are unpredictable and this unpredictability makes it impossible to prepare for unknown world events.

An example is the effects of Arab Spring and governmental changes in the last four years.

VUCA

Complexity

means that the chaotic nature of the world combined with the volatility and uncertainty of global events creates an environment of confusion and difficulty for today's leaders.

Ambiguity

means that there is a lack of clarity or transparency surrounding world events. It is hard to predict what threats are in the world if you do not know the who, what or why things are happening.

Howard Gardner, in his book, *Five Minds for the Future,* describes globalization as the movement of money, humanity, information and culture and the changes this is having on the identities of countries and the world as a whole.

Bethel in her book, *A New Breed of Leader* (2009), further describes the rapidly changing environment includes rapid pace of technology and information changes, globalization across the planet, religious radicalism, diasporas of people and culture and failing and emerging nations.

This multidimensional leadership chaos and organizational complexity creates challenges for today's leaders to lead effectively.

Leadership Challenges

A key leadership challenge is that people are no longer limited to ocean boundaries or imaginary lines drawn on a map to connect with other people. They reach out daily via the internet and social media to build a virtual nation.

They share ideas, thoughts and business projects globally. Interconnected people are the human capital of the new global organizations.

Another key leadership challenge is "We the people." People no longer want to be managed or motivated, they want to be inspired and desire a sense of purpose when they work. The concepts of freedom and liberty have spread across the globe assisted by the social consciousness of global interconnectedness as people share ideas and thoughts.

The leader of the future will need to connect at a heart, mind, body and soul level in order to tap into the potential of their people.

The last key leadership challenge then is what I call "Leader Shift." The old ways of the top-down command and control style leadership are waning and being replaced by a networked interconnectedness leadership style. In that top-down leadership style, all the power and corporate knowledge rested in the higher-ranked individual in an organization.

Today, because of corporate mergers, company buyouts, key personnel departures and the advent of the internet and power of social media, the true corporate power resides in their employee's global networking capability and the increasing value of the knowledge residing in their heads.

Reality Defined

Max De Pree (1989), in his book *Leadership is an Art* states that, "The first responsibility of a leader is to define reality, the last is to say thank you. In between, the leader is a servant" (p. 9). A leader defines reality by analyzing the challenges facing the organization and by understanding the scope, depth and breadth of the organizational leadership environment.

By analyzing and understanding the challenges, a long-term leadership strategy is needed for leadership development across all levels of leaders in organizations today. Leaders will face significant and complex challenges in the future leadership environment.

Executive Leadership Consultant

Since 1998 I have served in several military, non-profit, academic and professional organizations in the capacity of an executive leadership consultant, as well as a human capital strategist reporting to the CEO and the Board of Directors. My role as the executive leadership consultant focused on the growth and development of the people inside the organization.

I was responsible to the CEO to train, develop and mentor other leaders for future organizational roles, review training and development in the areas of leadership, technical competence, management and assess organizational processes and their effect on talent retention. I provided insight into how the people of the organization were functioning.

In my travels to visit local and worldwide organizations, I had the opportunity to travel to 35 different countries and to all 50 States. I had the opportunity to talk with junior employees and to CEOs about what we need in future leaders.

Based on my travels and discussions I have identified some key competencies and characteristics I believe a leader needs to have in today's uncertain and chaotic environment.

Competencies and Characteristics

Authentic with Integrity: Integrity first is an Air Force Core Value, but should be the number one value of all leaders. Authentic leaders model and maintain the values of the organization and act in a way that is both honest and trusting.

> **Authentic leaders are role models**

A leader who is open and honest today never has to remember the lie told yesterday. Authentic leader's words are true and credible and they live their core values daily.

Integrity + Respect = Trustworthiness

Authenticity means a leader is accountable and responsible for their actions, words and decisions.

Globally Interconnected: A leader must have a clear understanding of how technology, diversity, the redistribution of people on earth, failing nation-states and the interactions among diverse cultural groups affect organizations in a global market and global society. A leader must understand how to reach out via the internet, social media, technologically and through search engines to connect with people around the world.

Multi-Culturally Intelligent: A leader must be multi-culturally astute and understand how to work with peoples of different countries, cultures, religions and worldviews. A leader needs to be culturally smart and talented to use this cultural awareness to lead across barriers and generations and understand how to work with people of different countries and cultures.

I conducted a multinational leadership workshop in Kuwait with the Korean, Japanese and Australian Senior Enlisted Leaders. The workshop was focused on how to lead in a multinational and multicultural environment. Several topics were discussed, such as understanding cultural differences, leading multinational troops, language barriers and how to overcome them. The use of interpreters highlighted one of the main topics of language differences and how to overcome them.

Each leader was asked to explain their definition of leadership. Each leader defined leadership differently except where people and mission were concerned. The question highlighted to the audience how each senior leader viewed leadership and how their culture shaped their ideas.

After the workshop we created weekly meetings to bridge the culture gap between the multinational partners and to learn how to lead together. Each Wednesday, the senior leaders met for breakfast and took the time to share and learn about each partners' cultures, leadership style and military and social characteristics. This built a team that understood the cultural sensitivity and differences required to lead effectively and efficiently.

Creative and Critical Thinking: A leader needs to identify and evaluate information and then use the information to influence actions and decisions for the future. They need to engage in "out-of-the-box" synchronicity thinking and think at the tactical, operational and strategic level when looking at ambiguous and complex problems to develop innovative strategies and tactics.

A leader needs to be able to critically analyze problems and situations and foresee second, third and fourth order effects of proposed policies or actions. This requires thinking long term, being future-oriented and having a mental picture of what the organization should look like and be in the future.

Inspirational Visionary: An inspiring leader "breathes life" into the organization. A leader's vision creates a sense of purpose, inspires and motivates an organization. A leader must be able to build a clear and inspiring vision and be able to communicate it to their people or team. The vision should inspire and encourage their team with the vision of the organization's future.

The leader's vision provides clarity and focus to the organization. A leader must envision and communicate an inspiring vision and clearly define a strategy for the future. The leader creates strategies and initiatives that allow others to achieve the vision and accomplish current and future challenges and opportunities.

> **Leaders Inspire and Motivate**

Servant Leader: A true leader serves the people and the organization by rising above their own self-interests and embrace personal sacrifice and risk for the good of the organization and the team.

Create a Culture of Trust, Integrity and Respect: Trust is a vital component of a leader's success and is the very heart of a leader-follower relationship. An authentic leader is a role model for their people. A trustworthy leader builds a culture of integrity and respect and maintains trust with others. They interact with people unambiguously and respectfully. The relationship of the leader and the subordinate is a team relationship built on trust, respect and integrity.

Build Relationships and Alliances: Donald T. Phillips, in his book *Lincoln on Leadership*, describes the importance of building relationships and alliances. "Abraham Lincoln gained the trust and respect of his subordinates, building strong alliances on both the personal and professional level" (p. 27).

Leaders need to be masters at networking, relationships and alliance building. A leader understands that the relationship of the leader and their team is built on trust. They use leadership influence positively and skillfully to begin action and to influence actions. They enlarge and empower all team members to work together and across functional areas.

Furthermore, a leader needs to lead across multicultural and multinational boundaries to increase the effectiveness of the organization. Relationship building results in both personal and professional development. A leader needs

> **Leaders are masters at building teams**

to be able to build relationships with all people inside and outside the organization. A leader understands that a good team needs direction and growth to become a truly great team.

Lifelong Learner and Talent Developer: Be a lifelong learner who is agile, adaptive and reflective, that learns from experiences, training, development and successes and failures

A leader continuously develops, grows and reinvents themselves through continuous learning and development. They develop their replacements and look for the talent, skills, capability and leadership potential in their people. A leader is constantly looking for the talent, skills and potential in all people to develop and grow the necessary organizational talent for today and the challenges of the future.

This is important because each person has different goals, ideas, skills and potential. They take responsibility for developing professional expertise that adds value to organizational success.

Results and Outcomes Driven: A leader positively influences the moral element of an organization and determines the outcome of situations. They demonstrate the capability to act in an influential, urgent and steadfast way to realize outcomes and results. They remain focused on the organizational goals and leverage all available resources to achieve that goal.

A leader understands and can operate in a volatile, uncertain, complex and ambiguous world. They comprehend risk and manage it to achieve desired results. A leader encourages and rewards creativity, innovation and continuous improvement.

Lead Change with Agility: A leader must be able to improvise, adapt and overcome as rapidly as the current pace of change. They must be flexible and adaptive to quickly respond to crisis and to change. A leader maintains mission effectiveness during major changes in work tasks or work environment.

> **Leaders are Change Agents**

They recognize the need for change and efficiently manage both the change and the transition. They establish a solid change management plan and communicate frequently through the change to ensure the strategic themes and messages are conveyed.

Summary

The call for new leaders and leadership development is happening in society as a whole and in the military. The world around us has changed dramatically and drastically since the world has gone flat due to globalization and since the tragic events of 9/11.

This list of F(X) characteristics and competencies are those an F(X) leader needs to compete and survive in the VUCA or new normal environment. There are other characteristics and competencies you may feel are necessary and want to incorporate into your leadership or your organization's leadership development program.

Notes

_____

_____

_____

Key Takeaways

The world has changed

Developing yourself and your people will ensure you can survive and thrive in the future leadership environment.

Understand the global strategic picture

Look holistically at the changing world leadership environment. Understand the complexity and uncertainty so you can lead through challenges and opportunities.

Characteristics and Competencies are valuable

As a leader, you need to continually add capabilities and abilities to you leadership fitness. Characteristics and competencies provide you a plan for development.

Leadership Application

The following are 10 strategies for leading in a VUCA environment

- Develop flexible and adaptive thinking strategies
- Develop linear and non-linear thinking
- Learn how to look at the world holistically and strategically
- Become globally interconnected through social interactions
- Be a lifelong learner and learn new skills and talents to help you lead in the new normal
- Learn to communicate cross-functionally and multi-culturally
- Learn to make decisions at the pace of change
- Engage in "out-of-the-box" and synchronicity thinking
- Read and stay current on global trends and changes
- Learn to lead change quickly and responsively

Leadership Thought Questions

- How well are you prepared to lead in a VUCA environment?

- What leadership characteristics do you see in yourself as a leader?

- What leadership competencies do you need to develop?

- What are you currently learning to help you adapt your leadership skills?

F(X) Insight

- **Understand the changing leadership landscape**

- **Build a leaders-centric culture**

- **Trust is hard to gain but easy to lose**

- **Be a Servant Leader**

- **Lead change proactively**

- **Take responsibility for developing leadership**

- **Develop the organizational talent needed for a global environment**

Characteristics and Competencies Exercise

The purpose of this writing exercise is to write down your leadership characteristics and competencies. On a separate piece of paper, or on the lines below, write down your list of leadership characteristics and competencies that you feel you have and/or need. Use the lead-ins below to help you with this exercise.

- My leadership Competencies are:

- Leadership characteristics & competencies I need to develop are:

Notes

_____

_____

_____

_____

_____

_____

_____

_____

_____

F(X) Leadership Growth and Development Plan

After reading this chapter, review and reflect on the ideas and concepts presented. Think about how to integrate the ideas or concepts into one of the three growth and development areas--Personal, Professional or Leadership Competency. Think about what opportunities, challenges, resources or blind spots you may encounter when you begin your growth and development journey. Use the following questions to help you grow and develop.

1. What area will the ideas and concepts help me grow and develop?

    - Personal

    - Professional

    - Leadership

2. How will I incorporate this new talent or skill into my development?

3. What is my timeline for learning the new talent or skill?

4. What opportunity and resources exist for me to use this new talent or skill?

    - _____

    - _____

    - _____

5. What blind spots may derail me from using this new talent or skill?

    - _____

    - _____

    - _____

Chapter 5

Developing Your Plan

Key Leadership Concept:. The biggest challenge to a leadership growth and development plan is where do I start? You start by developing a yearly developmental plan and grow it into a long term life plan. A yearly plan allows you to express your vision for the next year, to define your specific goals and objectives and to commit yourself to continuous development and continuous growth actions.

How many times have you said: *My life is going nowhere…It feels like I am living a Groundhog Day everyday…I am not making a difference.* Wouldn't it be great if life allowed do-overs? Wouldn't it be great if you could go back in time and fix a mistake, redo an amazing moment in your life, or better yet, get out of a rut? Unfortunately, life is only lived once and it goes by quickly. If you find yourself not living the life you wanted, you still have time to make some changes in your life. You need to ask yourself a critical question.

What do I need to change in my life in order to live a better life?

We Must Change Ourselves

At the beginning of each new day, take the opportunity to start a portion of your life over by establishing new goals and new opportunities to change your life and to make an impact on those around you. Nevertheless, change is not easy and takes some perseverance and will power. Anything is possible if you are determined to make it happen. All change begins with you.

Dr. Viktor E. Frankl was an Austrian psychiatrist and neurologist who survived the Holocaust. In October 1944, Frankl and his wife Tilly were sent to Auschwitz concentration camp for internment. Soon after arriving at Auschwitz, Viktor was sent to another concentration camp called

Kaufering and his wife Tilly was sent to Bergen-Belsen. They would never see each other again and Tilly would die in the camp at the age of 24. Viktor's mom would be murdered in the gas chambers in Auschwitz and his brother would die in the same camp.

After being confined for three years and despite all the pain and suffering he endured, Dr. Viktor Frankl would write the book, *Man's Search for Meaning,* about his life in the concentration camp. In his book, two quotes stand out.

> "Between stimulus and response there is a space. In that, space is our power to choose our response. In our response lies our growth and our freedom."
>
> Viktor E. Frankl

"When we are no longer able to change a situation we are challenged to change ourselves" and "Everything can be taken from a man but one thing; the last of the human freedoms—to choose one's attitude in any given set of circumstances, to choose one's own way." To change you must want to change and you are responsible to change!

Never Give Up On Changing

On October 29, 1941, Winston Churchill spoke these words at Harrow School after having survived the first major air war called the Battle of Britain.

> This is the lesson: never give in, never give in, never, never, never, never—in nothing, great or small, large or petty—never give in except to convictions of honour and good sense. Never yield to force; never yield to the apparently overwhelming might of the enemy…There was no flinching and no thought of giving in; and by what seemed almost a miracle to those outside these Islands, though we ourselves never doubted it, we now find ourselves in a position where I say that we can be sure that we have only to persevere to conquer.

He was talking to students at Harrow School about never giving up in life despite all odds being against you. He challenged the students to never give up, to make an impact, and to persevere throughout their lives. Winston Churchill was setting the stage for the students to believe in themselves. The first step in making the impossible the possible is faith in your talents, gifts and mostly, faith in yourself.

What impact will your life have on others?
Are you ready to ignite and inspire your leadership?

Change Begins From Within

I start each year using the Stephen Covey philosophy of "Begin with the end mind." I usually start by asking two questions--What do I want to accomplish in the next year and where do I want to be next year? (e.g., location, occupation, education or situation) Once I answer these questions, I incorporate the Inspire and Retire Theorem, F(X) Models and the Leadership Based Mindset/Outcomes Model as a way to assess and adjust my progress as a leader.

The first step to becoming a better leader is to develop and implement a leadership development plan and strategy for your life. A plan and strategy begins first with an understanding of who you are. What skills, talents, experiences and attitude for learning do you possess and can you use them to build yourself up as a leader?

Purposeful development and self-assessment are keys to continual growth as a leader. Although this list of questions is not all conclusive, they can help you to determine what your leadership needs are. Furthermore, as you read the questions, other questions may come to mind that may help your leadership needs assessment to be completed. Write them down and answer them, too.

- Do I have a leadership development plan?
- Do I have the ability to organize ideas, resources and time effectively?
- Do I have the ability to make critical decisions?
- Do I have the ability to trust others and delegate work effectively?
- Do I have the desire to mentor, coach and teach my people?
- Do I have a strong desire to make an impact on my organization?
- Am I willing to take the initiative?
- Am I successful at building a team and developing their skills?
- Do I have the ability to develop leadership growth plans for my people?
- Can I give clear guidance to achieve goals?
- Can I influence others to achieve the organization's mission?
- Do I seek out opportunities to grow and develop my leadership skills?

After you determine your leadership needs, you need to develop a leader growth and development plan to achieve your leadership objectives. A leadership growth and development plan is a roadmap of where you are as a leader and where you want to go in your career and in life. As part of my growth and development plan I needed a strategy and a deliberate process to develop myself. I also needed a way of thinking about establishing and managing personal expectations and outcomes.

After reading *Effects-based Operations: Change in the Nature of War,* authored by Lieutenant General David A. Deptula (Retired), and first published by the Aerospace Education Foundation in 2001, I developed the Leadership Based Outcomes/Mindset Model and have used this model in my own life and in an Air Force Program called "Airmen's Time. The model for personal development is slightly different than the model I use for organizational development.

Leadership Based Outcomes/Mindset Model

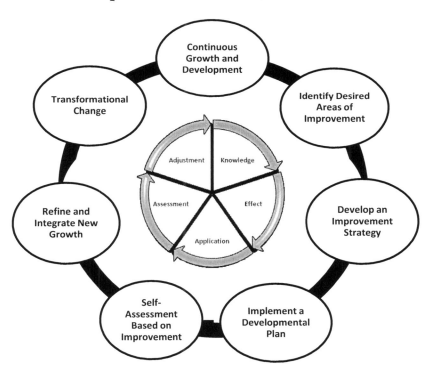

The five elements within the center consist of the following:

- Knowledge
- Effect
- Application
- Assessment
- Adjustment

Knowledge

The five-step process begins with the Knowledge stage which requires a comprehensive understanding of the Who you are as a person, professional and leader.

Effect

The Effect stage is where your development strategy and growth and development planning occur and is focused on desired future states or outcomes/mindset.

Application

The Application stage is where the actual execution of your development strategy takes place.

Assessment

The Assessment stage is focused on the impact of the effects on your three growth and development areas.

Adjustment

The Adjustment stage is where your strategy plan is validated and modified to produce new levels of knowledge in your personal, professional and leadership growth.

Continuously Reinventing Yourself

The outer seven elements of continuously reinventing yourself consist of the following:

- Identify Desired Areas of Improvement
- Develop an Improvement Strategy
- Implement a Development Plan
- Self-Assessment Based on Improvement
- Refine and Integrate New Growth
- Transformational Change
- Continuous Growth and Development

Identify Desired Areas of Improvement

The seven-element process begins with the Identify Desired Areas of Improvement stage, which requires self-awareness--Do I know all my talents, gifts, opportunities and capabilities? The first step in building my self-awareness is self-assessment.

I use the Strengths, Weaknesses, Opportunities and Threats (SWOT) analysis to help with my self-assessment.

SWOT Analysis

SWOT analysis is an organized development technique used to evaluate the Strengths, Weaknesses, Opportunities and Threats involved in a project or program, but is very helpful in personal growth and development, too.

After I complete the SWOT analysis I have a clearer understanding of myself and what opportunities and threats may help or improve my development.

With a clearer understanding I establish my goals and objectives for the year. A goal is an outcome or result you desire to achieve in your life or in your leadership.

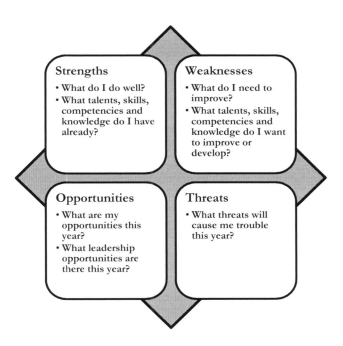

Strengths
- What do I do well?
- What talents, skills, competencies and knowledge do I have already?

Weaknesses
- What do I need to improve?
- What talents, skills, competencies and knowledge do I want to improve or develop?

Opportunities
- What are my opportunities this year?
- What leadership opportunities are there this year?

Threats
- What threats will cause me trouble this year?

Why Set Goals

- Goals are an essential part of developing and growing your leadership
- Goals provide focus and direction
- Goals provide a sense of accomplishment
- Goals identify desired outcomes and results

I like the S.MA.R^2.T model for establishing goals and objectives. The S.MA.R^2.T. or Specific, Measurable, Attainable, Relevant/Realistic and Time-Bound model is a structured tool that allows for a critical analysis of goals and how to achieve them.

S.M.A.R^2.T. goals are:

SPECIFIC

Specific means the goal needs to be as concrete as possible. Why do you want to achieve and accomplish the goal? Be as specific as possible to reduce ambiguity. Example: I want to improve my leadership skills by attending leadership seminars this year.

MEASURABLE

A measurable goal is tangible and quantifiable. Example: I want to improve my leadership skills by attending three leadership seminars this year.

ACTION-ORIENTED

Action-oriented goals mean that I will accomplish an activity that produces outcomes and results. Example: I will attend three leadership seminars this year to improve my leadership skills.

R^2 EALISTIC/RELEVANT

Realistic and Relevant goals are challenging but achievable and motivate you because they are important to you. Example: In order to be eligible for the supervisory position, I will attend three leadership seminars this year.

TIME-CONSTRAINED

Time constrained means there is a definable and a finite period of completion. Example: In order to be eligible for the supervisory position, I will attend three leadership seminars on March 22, June 15, and October 5, 2013.

Develop an Improvement Strategy

Once I can answer these questions, I can move on to the Develop an Improvement Strategy. This stage is where I develop my change strategy and focus on what desired effects, future states or outcomes I want to develop or change in the next year. This is the true essence of F(X) leadership. What do I need to do to create the effects or outcomes in my life or leadership that I desire.?

Implement a Development Plan

This stage is where the actual execution of the growth and development strategies takes place in order for change to happen.

Self-Assessment Based on Improvement

The Assessment stage focuses on the impact of the change by assessing the results of the effects on my daily life. This is my map and compass stage. This stage is also where I assess my plan's effectiveness against the milestones and timelines I have laid into the plan. This lets me know where I am going and how I know when I get there.

Refine and Integrate New Growth

This stage is where my change strategies are implemented to produce new levels of knowledge of self-awareness.

Transformational Change

This stage is where all the hard work has paid off. Your outcome has been achieved and you have acquired a new skill, talent or mindset to help you continue to grow and develop in your three growth areas.

Continuous Growth and Development

This stage is where you begin to evaluate yourself again to find out what other skills, talents or mindsets you need to acquire after you have grown in an area. Using the F(X) model you can grow and develop yourself and become a better leader.

<u>Sample</u>

<u>12 Month Growth and Development Plan</u>

I. Personal Leadership--Building and Discovering Self
- Participate in a year-long physical fitness program to improve my physical well-being
- Live my life in balance: Spiritual, Social, Physical and Emotional
- Read four books about self-improvement this year
- Take a personal assessment this year to improve self-awareness (.i.e., DISC, MBTI, Big Five, CPI 260 Instrument)
- Request leadership feedback from my mentor every quarter

II. Professional Competency
- Seek one new career improvement opportunity through advanced education and/or professional certification
- Mentor subordinates quarterly to increase their career knowledge
- Develop two new strategic alliances in the organization to increase my organizational leadership
- Attend two career development workshops in April and in August

III. Leadership Competency
- Be a Mentor for one new person this year
- Lead by example and set the standard everyday
- Seek one new leadership opportunity in professional and community organizations this year
- Read four leadership books or biographies of leaders this year
- Attend leadership seminars and workshops (i.e., John Maxwell

Summary

Finally, why change? At the end of your life you should never look back in regret saying I should have, I wish I had, or maybe if…what you should say is, "Wow, what a ride…can I do it again?" Each of us is given only a finite amount of time; the choice is yours to waste it or make an impact with it. Those who have felt the bitter taste of defeat understand and know what it takes to achieve victory and will continue to change and struggle until they have won. However, those who never try, who never get out of their comfort zone, or who just settle for second best will never live an amazing life. Now, go out and change your life!

Key Takeaways

You must be a catalyst for change

Growing and developing yourself begins from an inward desire to change. You must be your own change agent.

Purposeful development is the key to continuous growth

Growth and development are not a one-time event, they are continuous and deliberate.

Determine your outcome and effects

Take the initiative and determine your leadership and life needs, then implement your strategy.

Leadership Application

The following are 10 strategies for developing your plan:

- Establish your leadership plan every year

- Establish goals that are achievable but stretch your leadership

- Use the Leadership Based Outcomes/Mindset Model to assess and adjust your strategy

- Establish a leadership strategy with a desired end state so you know what you are striving to achieve in your life

- Life is finite, don't waste your days on trivial pursuits

- Never give up on yourself, believe in your potential

- Use the S.W.O.T. model to establish your effects and outcomes

- Improve each competence area

- Refine and integrate your change strategies as you develop yourself

- Failure is only a setback not a final outcome

Leadership Thought Questions

- Are you willing to take the initiative to grow and develop?

- What areas of development do you need to work on this year?

- What is stopping you from taking your life seriously?

F(X) Insight

- **Establish a leadership plan**

- **Establish S.M.A.R.^{2}T Goals**

- **Discover and understand your strengths, weakness, threats and opportunities**

- **Use assessment tools to discover your potential**

- **Reach out and find a mentor who can help you grow**

- **Take your development seriously**

- **Understand how to develop yourself in a disciplined and methodical way**

- **Learn from your successes and setbacks**

Growth and Development Exercise

The purpose of this writing exercise is to determine what areas of growth and development you need to improve and develop. On a separate piece of paper, or the lines below, write down your list of skills, talents or mindset that you feel you need to improve yourself and to be prepared for future challenges.

Notes

_____

_____

_____

_____

_____

_____

_____

_____

_____

_____

F(X) Leadership Growth and Development Plan

After reading this chapter, review and reflect on the ideas and concepts presented. Think about how to integrate the ideas or concepts into one of the three growth and development areas--Personal, Professional or Leadership Competency. Think about what opportunities, challenges, resources or blind spots you may encounter when you begin your growth and development journey. Use the following questions to help you grow and develop.

1. What area will the ideas and concepts help me grow and develop?

   - Personal

   - Professional

   - Leadership

2. How will I incorporate this new talent or skill into my development?

3. What is my timeline for learning the new talent or skill?

4. What opportunity and resources exist for me to use this new talent or skill?

   - _____

   - _____

   - _____

5. What blind spots may derail me from using this new talent or skill?

   - _____

   - _____

   - _____

PART TWO

People-Focused F(X)

As a leader you have an opportunity to make an impact on your organization and your people. A great leader understands that any achievements they achieve are due to the people of the team they lead. A great leader then is always looking out for their people's best interest. A leader is a visionary person who inspires others to follow their lead and has the capability to make everyone in the organization feel unique. A successful leader uses a broad brush and paints the strategic picture for their people. Through this strategic painting the leader charts the course for everyone to follow and captures the heart of the people. People enjoy coming to work with a boss who inspires them, develops them daily and makes them feel a part of the team.

"As Iron sharpens Iron so does one person sharpen another."

Proverbs 27:17

Chapter 6

Inspire or Retire!

> **Key Leadership Concept**: Inspire your people, your team and your organization to great heights of professional growth and mission accomplishment or retire so another leader can inspire them. An inspirational leader inspires people to greatness through positive influence and encouragement. Inspired people reach greater heights of performance, creativity and innovation in an organization.

The art and science of leadership is something I have studied since I attended my first military leadership school in 1988. Today, I continue to study, develop and grow my leadership skills through daily application and a regime of continuous learning and development. Some of my favorite authors are Jack Welch, Stephen Covey, Ken Blanchard, James C. Hunter, Donald T. Phillips and John Maxwell.

My Personal Journey

My leadership journey began when I packed my suitcase and left Tucson, Arizona, for the green, green grass of Basic Military Training at Lackland Air Force Base, San Antonio, Texas. I was assigned to the 3701st Basic Military Training Squadron and the squadron's motto was, **"Lead, Follow or Get the Hell out of the Way."** This inspiring motto has stuck with me my entire career and it has kept me focused as a leader. As I have progressed in my career, I reduced the motto to three simple words – **Inspire or Retire.**

Inspirational Leadership + Motivated People = a team with outstanding mission accomplishments

I have shaped my leadership style by combining both the aspects of Transformational and Inspirational leadership. Transformational leadership involves developing individuals by tapping into their sources of inspiration, innovation, creativity and drive to create a better future for organizations.

Transformational leadership is a way of leading in which the leader is a learner, a mentor and a teacher. The leader is a trailblazer, guide and pioneer. The leader is not only concerned with improving conditions within existing frameworks and mindsets, but with going one step further to design and lead processes that shift the frameworks and mindsets themselves.

Today, the real key to leadership is leading with your people. People are looking for leaders who inspire them. They are looking for meaning and purpose not trophies and awards. When authentic leaders inspire people, they reach new levels of innovation, achievement and commitment.

Leaders that Inspire Me

Brigadier General Joshua Chamberlain

On October 3, 1889, General Joshua L. Chamberlain said these inspiring words at the dedication of the Maine Monuments at Gettysburg Battlefield Cemetery:

> The inspiration of a noble cause involving human interests wide and far enables men to do things they did not dream themselves capable of before, and which they were not capable of alone. The consciousness of belonging, vitally, to something beyond individuality; of being part of a personality that reaches we know not where, in space and time, greatens the heart to the limits of the soul's ideal, and

Inspire or Retire

Alfred Lansing's book titled, *Endurance: Shackleton's Incredible Voyage* is one of my favorite books on inspirational leadership. It shows a leader who overcomes life's obstacles to bring his team home alive.

It also shows that great leadership and great teams can overcome the odds together.

The skills that a team needs are great leadership, continuous communication, inspiring optimism, and absolute determination.

Inspiring optimism is a force multiplier.

builds out the supreme of character…In great deeds something abides. On great fields something stays. Forms change and pass; bodies disappear; but spirits linger, to consecrate ground for the vision-place of souls. And reverent men and women from afar, and generations that know us not and that we know not of, heart-drawn to see where and by whom great things were suffered and done for them, shall come to this deathless field, to ponder and dream; and lo! The shadow of a mighty presence shall wrap them in its bosom, and the power of the vision pass into their souls…This is the great reward of service, to live, far out and on, in the life of others.

He was talking about the reward of service before self, in the ability to live your life – far beyond your own life – through service to others and as an inspiration to others. For Brigadier General Chamberlain and the 20th Maine, their service before self helped preserve America during the Civil War. They fought for a noble cause and an idea larger than themselves.

A1C Elizabeth Nicole Jacobsen

A1C Elizabeth Nicole Jacobson lived and died for that same inspiration of a noble cause. On 28 September 2005, while serving as a Gun Truck Weapons Operator for Convoy operations at Camp Bucca, Iraq, A1C Jacobson was killed when her Gun Truck was struck by an improvised explosive device or IED. She was the first female Security Forces Member to die in Iraq and was awarded the Purple Heart and the Bronze Star posthumously. The citation for her Bronze Star reads:

Airman First Class Elizabeth N. Jacobson distinguished herself by meritorious achievement as a gun truck crew served weapons operator for convoy operations 586th Expeditionary Security Forces Squadron, 586th Expeditionary Mission Support Group, 386th Expeditionary Wing, United States Central Command Air Forces, while engaged in ground operations against opposing armed forces at Camp Bucca, Iraq, on 28 September 2005. On that date while providing lead security on a convoy mission to Navistar on the border of Iraq and Kuwait, her vehicle was struck by an improvised explosive device. Airman Jacobsen gave her life in defense of our nation and for the freedom of the people of Iraq. By her heroic actions and unselfish dedication to duty in the service of her country, Airmen Jacobson has reflected great credit upon herself and the United States Air Force.

In the short 21 years A1C Jacobson was on this earth, she touched many hearts and lives. She was a true role model and mentor for all people who served in uniform. She lived the core values. A1C Jacobson lived Article 1 of the Code of Conduct in actions and deeds that states, "I am an American, fighting in the Forces which Guard my Country and our way of life. I am prepared to give my life in their Defense." She understood these words and ultimately gave her life for our Country and our Way of Life. She was and still is an inspiration for me.

Inspire or Retire Theorem

The Inspire or Retire Theorem wraps up the F(X) Leadership framework. From the beginning of the book, you have learned that by continuously developing, growing and reinventing yourself you are the key to your leadership.

What if the leaders in your organization

- Knew the organizational vision, goals, values and the impact their leadership had on the success of the organization

- Knew success as a leader included knowing themselves, their team and the organization

- Knew a leader must have high moral and ethical values and that character counts

- Knew leaders are responsible for their actions and their words

- Knew they needed to continuously develop, grow and reinvent themselves to meet the challenges of the future

- Understood their role in developing other leaders

- Understood character, courage, commitment and communication are key components of leadership

- Understood they are responsible for their leadership development

- Understood they are the key to their leadership

The Inspire or Retire Theorem answers all the above questions in a mathematical mnemonic that encapsulates my leadership responsibility to the people I led and the organization I served. It was designed as a visual representation for me to remember to always **Inspire or Retire**.

Senior Management

$$\int f^{(x)} (P + OM) + \left[\frac{RE^{(LxE)} + L\,(360°) + DL^{(10X)} + R}{(CV \times OV)} \right] + OR^{(MxVxSPxP)} = BL^{(C4I)}$$

Yes → Inspire

No → Retire

Junior Employee

The first part of the Theorem is a reminder that from the Junior Employee to Senior Management, leadership is everyone's business. In a VUCA environment where organizations are flatter, have a networked interconnectedness leadership style and are globally interconnected, the pace of change is exponentially faster. Everyone must lead in today's organization.

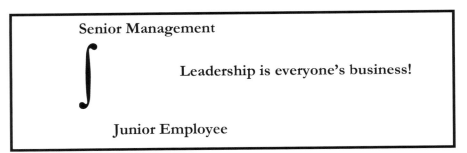

Senior Management

$\int$

Leadership is everyone's business!

Junior Employee

The Theorem further states that the overall function – or the $F^{(X)}$ of every leader – is to lead and inspire People (P) and execute the Organizational Mission (OM). Since people are not things, we lead them, not manage them to lead.

$F^{(X)}$ (P + OM)

Lead People and Execute the Mission

The bottom part of the equation is the fusion of your personal core values (CV) and the organization's core values (OV). This is a key and foundational organizational principle. It is the fusion or synchronization of the combined values, beliefs and tenets of you and the organization. It is a melding of your leadership and the leadership expectations of the organization.

> # (CV x OV)
>
> ## A fusion of your
> ## core values and the values of the organization

As a leader of people in your organization, it is your responsibility to lead by example $RE^{(LxE)}$ and set the standard for your people. Using a 360-degree leadership approach ($L (360^\circ)$), you can maximize your leadership potential by realizing that you can lead anyone, anytime and anywhere in an organization and in your life.

To help build the organizational leadership bench in your organization and to help maximize the potential of your people, use the John Maxwell concept of developing people as leaders ($DL (10X)$) to increase the organizational leadership capacity by 10-fold.

Finally, as a leader, you need to build resiliency in your life and those you lead so they are well balanced and able to perform at their maximum potential. Resiliency (TPMS) (Technically, Physically, Mentally, Spiritually).

> # $(RE^{(LxE)} +L (360^\circ) +DL^{(10X)} +R^{(TPMS)})$
>
> ## Lead by example with 360-degree approach

After compiling the inner equation, you need to have a holistic understanding of the Organization's (OR) Mission (M) x Vision (V) x Strategic Plan (SP) x Priorities (P) in order to develop and Build Leaders (BL) with Character, Competence, Courage, Commitment and Innovation (C4I) to continue the growth and development of leaders for the organization.

> # $OR^{(MxVxSPxP)} = BL^{(C4I)}$
>
> ## Understand the Organization and Build Leaders

An inspirational leader envisions and communicates an inspiring vision and establishes a strategy for the future. They inspire and encourage their team by setting a trail and allowing their people to take the lead in accomplishing that vision and involve their team in identifying and achieving common goals.

A leader creates strategies and initiatives that allow others to achieve the vision and effectively manages current and future challenges and opportunities. An inspirational leader must lead in this VUCA environment.

The most significant contribution we can make as leaders today is to leave a legacy of inspired leaders behind to take care of tomorrow. We can leverage our skills, talents and experiences to transform our people into leaders.

Summary

As leaders, we need to examine ourselves to see if we are inspiring our people to greater heights of performance and success. Inspirational leadership is leading by example and through words like, "You did a great job today!" Alternatively, my favorite, "I am proud of you!" Remember when you no longer can inspire your people to greatness and it becomes more of an effort to lead each day, then you need to move aside and allow someone else to lead.

Notes

_____

_____

_____

_____

_____

_____

_____

Key Takeaways

Be an inspirational leader

Inspirational leader's empower and unleash their people's creativity, innovation and collaboration.

No bystanders allowed

Be an engaged leader and understand your people and your organization. Leadership is everyone's business.

Lead Follow or Get the Hell out of the Way

When you can no longer be the leader who molds, shapes, and inspires then it is time to move out of the way.

Leadership Application

The following are 10 strategies for becoming an inspirational and transformational leader:

- Be a role model by living out your authentic leadership daily
- Create a vision and shared purpose that people can rally around
- Stimulate and encourage creativity in your people
- Respect and celebrate each individual team member's contribution
- Provide open and honest relationships across the organization
- Build a culture that opens the door to creativity and collaboration
- Live values that connect with people's heart, mind, body and soul
- Create open and transparent lines of communication
- Institute a leadership environment that has trust, respect and dignity as its foundation
- Be willing to inspire or retire

Leadership Thought Questions

- Whom are you inspiring with your leadership?

- How could you use the Inspire or Retire Theorem in your role as a leader?

- Who inspires you as a leader?

- How could your organization use the Inspire or Retire Theorem in developing leaders?

- What did you learn in this chapter?

- What significant ideas or points stand out in your mind?

- What ideas or points can you apply to your development?

F(X) Insight

- **Leaders inspire!**

- **Leaders encourage**

- **The best way to lead is to teach, mentor and coach**

- **Leave a legacy of inspired leaders**

- **Leader's actions shout louder than their words**

- **When in doubt, lead!**

- **Understand the values of your organization**

- **Leaders are fully engaged with their people**

Reflective Exercise

Take time to reflect on an inspirational leader in your life. How did they inspire you and how did it change your life. Take your time to reflect and see how their leadership affected your life.

My Inspirational Leader

One of the greatest inspirational leaders in my life was my father. My father was not a great leader of industry or a great military leader. Nevertheless, he did serve our country honorably as an Army Sergeant in Korea. My Dad did two things that inspired me and made me who I am today. First, he adopted me when he married my Mom and then called me his son. Second, he taught me what it means to want to live each day to its fullest as if it was your last. In the last year of his life, my father inspired me in his actions and his words as he battled cancer.

As I watched my Dad slowly die from the effects of cancer on his body, I learned a lot about faith, what being a family really means, and what real courage is when faced with an overwhelming trial.

My father and I spoke a lot in that last year of his life and although we talked about many things and many of his experiences in life, the greatest words of inspiration my Dad left to me before he died was, "I am proud of you." My father passed away on May 20, 1996, from cancer a year after I pinned on Master Sergeant. He inspired me to reach beyond my dreams.

F(X) Leadership Growth and Development Plan

After reading this chapter, review and reflect on the ideas and concepts presented. Think about how to integrate the ideas or concepts into one of the three growth and development areas--Personal, Professional or Leadership Competency. Think about what opportunities, challenges, resources or blind spots you may encounter when you begin your growth and development journey. Use the following questions to help you grow and develop.

1. What area will the ideas and concepts help me grow and develop?

   - Personal

   - Professional

   - Leadership

2. How will I incorporate this new talent or skill into my development?

3. What is my timeline for learning the new talent or skill?

4. What opportunity and resources exist for me to use this new talent or skill?

   - _____

   - _____

   - _____

5. What blind spots may derail me from using this new talent or skill?

   - _____

   - _____

   - _____

Chapter 7

Know Your People

> **Key Leadership Concept:** There is no leadership without followers. Leadership requires that you know your people and continue to build the relationship you have with your subordinates or followers.

L eadership is all about people, therefore, all leadership is relational. Kouzes & Posner (2006), in their book *Leadership Challenge*, defines leadership as, "Leadership is a relationship between those who aspire to lead and those who choose to follow" (p. 52).

As a leader your primary mission is to grow and develop your people. Your goal is to help them grow and develop as leaders in your organization in the same way you are developing. A leader who invests the time and patience to grow an emerging leader into an enduring leader reaps the benefit of increased organizational leadership capacity.

Engaged Leadership

Leading and developing others is engaged leadership. It requires attention to detail and engaged leaders. Engaged leadership is direct leader involvement with your people and it requires leader and follower accountability and responsibility. Every leader is accountable and responsible for their people and the success of their team.

Today more than ever, it is important for leaders to be engaged with their people. If a leader stays engaged with their people, they understand they are a part of the team and the company. People with engaging leaders tend to feel that their opinions count and they are important.

My Experience

It has been my experience that if I remained engaged on a daily basis with my co-workers, my subordinates and my boss, then communication flows freely, trust continues and everyone is on the same page. Also, based on my experience, my subordinates are more innovative and productive when I treat them as people and not just workers.

Disengaged leaders create disunity and mistrust because communication is scarce and there is a lack of caring on behalf of the leader. An engaged leader is not only responsible for the output of the team but also the mentoring and development of the team.

Trust Is Key!

To be an effective leader, people need to trust you and believe in you. Your walk and your talk need to match. In his book *The 8th Habit: From Effectiveness to Greatness*, Stephen Covey says, "Trust is the key to all relationships." Relationships are held together by a level of trust and mutual respect that each person in the relationship has for one another." A person of genuine and authentic character is trustworthy.

John Maxwell, in his book *21 Irrefutable Laws of Leadership* says, leadership is about "Influence – nothing more and nothing less". Leadership is about influencing people to follow your lead and to accomplish the mission.

It is all about building and sustaining relationships. In addition, relationships are built upon trust and respect which is all about your character. Ultimately, your character and your leadership are one. You cannot lead effectively without a genuine character. A leader needs insight into how they operate, how they make decisions and how to treat people in order to lead people. Our character can be an asset or a liability depending on how well we know and understand ourselves.

Motivation

Leaders must work to keep their people motivated if they plan to keep their talent. Organizational leaders know talented employees stay with companies that inspire and motivate them. People want to feel a part of something that is important and will make a difference.

Motivation is the drive from inside a person. "Put simply, motivation is what causes people to behave as they do." (Denhardt, Denhardt and Aristigueta, 2009, p. 146).

Motivation is a leadership challenge because as a leader you have no control over what motivates your people. What may motivate one person may not motivate someone else. A leader must influence, mentor and guide their personnel daily and can look for ways to motivate them but ultimately they are responsible to be motivated. Motivation causes people to achieve more than they thought they could possibly do.

Motivation is a key organizational driver in keeping their employees motivated and focused on the mission. Understanding how to influence people and help them meet their internal needs can produce effective mission results.

Knowledge-Enabled People

With the globalization of the world economies, the rate and pace of change, new emerging technologies and the chaotic nature of the world today, organizations are reliant on knowledge-enabled and globally connected employees to remain competitive.

Organizations need knowledge-enabled leaders and highly competent employees. Therefore, it is an organizational imperative you invest in developing your people systematically and persistently. Developing leaders in a deliberate process guarantees you will produce the requisite leadership for the future.

By growing and developing your people, you are building a leadership bench for your team and your organization. This is an organizational imperative and a necessity. These are the principles of continuous development, continuous coaching and continuously encouraging your people.

People-Focused Leadership

People-focused leadership involves setting and clarifying organizational and developmental leadership expectations. Letting your people know what you and the organization expects of them in the area of growth and development is important.

Your people need to own their leadership development and understand their importance in the organization and how you plan to invest in them. This information will communicate trust, develop responsibility and it will reinforce the importance of growth and development to the organization.

People-Focused Leadership

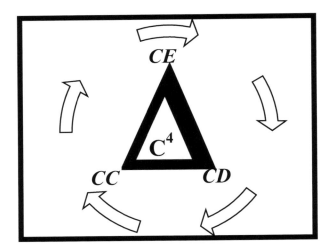

Δ	• The Greek symbol DELTA represents change or difference. Change as an emeriging leader is a constant.
C4	• Character, Competence, Courage and Commitment -- C4 is the most explosive part of the function of (x) because it represents who your people are deep down inside, their abilities, strengths and passions.
CD	• Continuous Development -- As a leader you must continually develop your people professionally, technically, mentally, spiritually and physically to develop new skills, new capabilities, new passions and a new mindset.
CC	• Continuous Coaching -- Your leadership coaching in this process will help your people understand the importance, breadth, depth and context of leadership development.
CE	• Continuous Encouragement -- As a leader you must continue to praise and encourage your people so they stay on the leading edge and help improve the organization.

By establishing expectations for your people, you empower them to take ownership of their development and ensure they know they are an important organizational asset.

Teach, Coach and Mentor

When I am building leaders, I look for growth and development three levels down. First, I look at the growth and development of the individual I am mentoring.

Are they following their plan and developing themselves? Do I see an increase in their self-confidence and their leadership responsibility?

Second, I look at the growth and development of the people the individual is leading. Are they coaching and teaching their people? Are they taking the time to grow and develop the next generation of leaders? Are they helping others to succeed? Are they building stronger relationships with their people and their teams?

Third, I look at the individual's people to see if they have adopted the culture of learning and leadership. Do they desire to grow and develop and take accountability for their own development?

If I can see three levels of development and growth, then the F(X) leadership model is working correctly. F(X) leaders teach, coach and mentor to produce more leaders.

Teach

The principal purpose of a teacher is to educate and to transfer information and bestow knowledge on their apprentice or trainee. As the teacher, you need to teach the skills, knowledge and aptitudes essential to accomplish the job successfully.

Your role as the teacher means that you outline the fundamental parts of the task to perform and to impart the information to the trainee. Provide step-by-step instructions that involves your trainee doing the tasks or procedures. On the job training is your most effective teaching tool.

Coach

The principal purpose of coach is to sharpen career and leadership skills and give direction on how to improve those skills. Your role is to challenge your employee to execute to the best of their ability and as independently as possible. As the coach you help your employee/apprentice to develop professional and leadership expertise and set realistic and achievable goals.

You encourage and provide the necessary leadership to grow and develop the apprentice for the mission today, but also the challenges of the future. Coaching helps you grow a Junior employee into a productive member of the team and sets them up for future success.

Mentor

The name mentor is derived from Homer's epic poem the Odyssey. Mentor, an old friend of King Odysseus, is left in charge of the King's son Telemachus, when he goes to fight the Trojan wars. Through the teaching of Mentor, Telemachus grows to Manhood and assist his father in reclaiming his kingdom.

Mentoring focuses on developing the whole person and is a collaborative relationship in which a leader with more experience and knowledge mentors another person. A mentor is one who is willing to share their skills, knowledge and expertise to grow and develop another person.

To build a collaborative relationship, you need to demonstrate respect and trust for the individual you are developing personally, professionally and in their leadership role. As a mentor you are a role model for the individual to emulate. You need to be a living example of the values, ethics, leadership and professional principles that you want the individual to inculcate.

By setting and clarifying your expectations early, you can help develop enthusiastic employees and position your organization to outperform its peers. One method of setting and clarifying expectations is through a growth and development plan. People-focused leadership only occurs with decisive and purposeful action on the part of the leader to establish an authentic relationship with their people in order to grow and develop them.

Growth and Development Plan

A growth and development plan is a way for you to set and clarify expectations for your people. It helps you and the organization chart out what you want your employees to learn and add to their professional and leadership competency. It is a tool to clearly define career and personal development goals.

Clarifying

Discover as much as possible about the person. Understand how they see the world, how the make decisions, discover their potential roadblocks and derailers and see how they interact with people. Use assessment tools like MBTI and the 360 mirror to help in clarifying the person's leadership. Talk to subordinates, peers and bosses to fill in any gaps.

Setting Goals

Help your people set goals that are realistic and achievable and meet their desired outcomes in their life and leadership. Use the same S.M.A.R^2.T model that was described earlier in this book.

You need to take the time to align the leadership growth and development plan so it aligns with the individual's needs and the needs of the organization. The growth and development plan is for you and the employee to develop together. It is your job as the leader to equip your people for future success in the organization. The form is an example of a leadership growth and development plan.

S.M.A.R^2.T

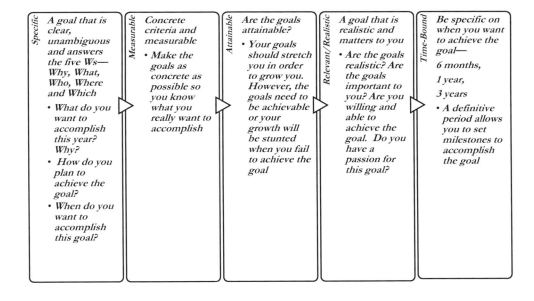

Leadership Growth and Development Plan	
Name:	**Supervisor:**
Job Position:	**Date:**
Date in Current Position:	**Vision & Mission Statement:**
Section A: Personal Development	
<u>**Short-Term Career Goals (1-2 years)**</u>	
<u>**Long-Term Career Goals (3-5 years)**</u>	
Section B: Professional Development	
<u>**Short-Term Career Goals (1-2 years)**</u>	
<u>**Long-Term Career Goals (3-5 years)**</u>	
Section C: Leadership Development	
Short-Term Career Goals (1-2 years)	
Long-Term Career Goals (3-5 years)	

Develop your people through constant dialogue, feedback and assessment. Feedback is a business mechanism we use to share information on performance, learning and goal achievement. Dialogue is more of a human interaction method of sharing information, ideas, points of view and connecting at the human level versus the professional level.

Dialogue helps build trust, respect and lets your people know you care about them as people and not just as workers. Assessment identifies areas needing improvement and areas that have grown. This helps the leader and follower to assess the leadership growth plan and identify potential areas to work on for the next 6 months to a year.

As a teacher, coach and mentor you need to build up employee commitment and confidence to drive greater performance. You need to develop individual skills, talents and abilities to grow the next generation of leaders. Finally, you inspire and guide others by sharing your knowledge, experiences and wisdom to shape and mold the individual to help them achieve their goals.

Follower Development Cycle

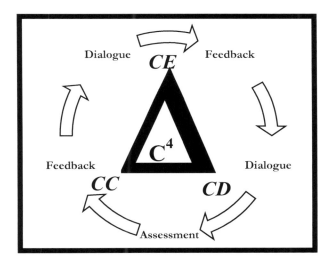

The Follower Development Cycle relies on constant dialogue, feedback and assessment and leadership to grow and develop your people and build a solid team. In the book *Leader to Leader*, Bennis (1999), explains if you allow your team members to use their strengths, you can move them around and create a more effective, more nimble leadership group.

These positive norms are reflected in cooperation and in individuals working together. The People-Focused Leadership and Follower Development Cycle reinforce the F(X) Leadership Competencies of Create a Culture of Trust, Integrity and Respect and Build Relationships and Alliances. A leader needs to continue building the relationships through feedback and dialogue to reinforce trust and respect to enlarge and empower their people and team.

Investing in other people is a key aspect of the F(X) Leadership Model. Building leaders assists others in their development and allows you to be a servant leader by helping them grow.

C-Level Development

The Inspire or Retire Theorem has kept me focused in my coaching and mentoring relationships. It has provided me with a constant reminder that I am developing leaders not followers and that it is about helping others achieve their desired outcomes and goals in life. Over that past 12 years I have had the opportunity to help numerous people achieve their goals, desired outcomes in life and their desired career goals.

Each person I had the opportunity to work with had different life goals and different developmental plans. However, each had the desire to grow and develop to become a better person, a better professional and a better leader. The case studies below are a select few I have worked with who achieved their goals to become C-level leaders.

Cathy

Cathy was a mid-level IT Professional and technical expert in her field when I met her. During our first counseling session, she expressed a desire to achieve more in her life and a desire to advance in her career field. After a series of discovery, questions concerning her present growth and development plan, it became evident that she spent most of her time developing her technical competence and allowed her personal and leadership competence to atrophy. Working together, we set up a new plan to balance her competence areas.

Since her personal and leadership competence areas lacked development for several years, one of the first actions for her growth and development was a series of personality and learning assessments. This information helped to discover her personality type and learning tactics in order to develop a growth and development plan and to reduce potential leadership derailers and roadblocks to her development.

Another developmental assessment was a 360 mirror to discover what her peers, subordinates and bosses thought about her as a leader and a professional. The mirror feedback provided further information that was helpful in designing her plan in areas that were assessed low. We combined these three assessment tools to develop her plan to grow and develop.

The plan concentrated her development in her personal and leadership competence areas while maintaining her professional and technical competence. Her plan emphasized interpersonal communications and relationship building, strategic leadership development, organizational or community leadership roles and mentoring.

Over three years, Cathy followed her plan and developed herself on a daily basis. Based on her growth and development she was promoted to be the division chief. Her disciplined approach to self-development and developing others helped her be promoted to the Chief Learning Officer for her organization.

Sean

Sean was an average firefighter with an enormous amount of energy and enthusiasm but was having difficulty achieving his goal of Fire Chief. During our first counseling session it became evident that what he was missing in his development was challenging work assignments that displayed his ability to lead. He was technically competent and personally competent, but his leadership development was not to the level he needed to advance.

Based on his boss' feedback his leadership skills were in question because he had not been fully tested as a leader. Sean had tactical and operational leadership skills and could lead personnel into a fire and take charge of situations but did not have the "big picture" of the Fire Department.

We developed his growth and development plan around strategic leadership skills, fire education courses and leadership roles in the community outreach program on fire prevention. His development also included mentoring from other Fire Chiefs to increase his understanding of the role of Fire Chief.

Sean developed quickly and studied relentlessly to achieve his goal. His senior leadership provided a series of opportunities and assignments to increase his strategic understanding of the Fire Department and growth and development as a leader. Eighteen months after he started a disciplined approach to development, he was promoted to Fire Chief. Because of his enthusiasm and leadership as a Fire Chief, he was asked to become the Director of the Fire Academy 2 years later.

Craig

Craig was an IT Project Manager working for the U.S. Government and was considered a "fast burner." He was achieving success quickly in the organization and was viewed as a potential candidate for executive leadership development. When I met him he was frustrated about not achieving a recent promotion and not happy with the recent feedback from his boss. I had the opportunity to coach him during the trying times and evaluated what his boss had actually said to him in their feedback session.

His boss indicated that he was moving too fast and not taking the time to learn the organizations' business. He needed to get experience in the organization before he would be considered for another promotion. Craig had the head knowledge and the charisma but lacked a clear understanding of the function and role of the organization.

His development plan was designed to increase his knowledge of the federal organization and the promotion criteria of the organization. The plan focused around the knowledge, skills and aptitudes required for the organization and further advancement. His plan also emphasized his need for strategic leadership skills, interpersonal skills, goal setting and team building skills.

Craig applied himself to his development and slowed himself down to gain the experience he needed to understand the organization. He grew over a period of 4 years and acquired the necessary experience and strategic outlook of the organization to get promoted. After a series of organizational assignments, each with increased responsibility, he was promoted to Chief Program Officer.

Summary

As a leader, you cannot build and grow others without first developing the knowledge, skills and aptitudes required to fully use that leadership. The same can be said about delegating responsibility to lead others without training, development and the experience of leading themselves first. With today's technology and global changes an organizational leader needs to be constantly learning to stay relevant. Developing other leaders is a critical leadership skill in any organization.

It is also a trust relationship between the organization and their people. A leader has been entrusted with the organization's most valuable, and at times, scarcest asset—their talented people.

An organization that delegates the responsibility to lead others without proper preparation sets up the conditions for failure for the new supervisor. However, an organization who fails to empower a capable leader causes frustration. Only a properly prepared leader should be entrusted to lead others

Key Takeaways

Be a teacher, mentor and coach to your people

Shape expectations and inspire your people by being a teacher, mentor and coach. Develop your people to be leaders.

Understand your people's needs and desires

Know your people well—their needs, desires and capabilities to grow and develop them.

Leadership Application

The following are 10 strategies for developing your people:

- Focus on the critical role leadership plays in developing people and executing the organization's operations

- Highlight important attributes, traits or aspects of your team and your people

- Create opportunities to improve your people's leadership capacity and capability

- Implement and improve programs designed to develop leaders

- Encourage and facilitate leadership encounters between leaders and their employee

- Identify opportunities for improvement, as well as problems, weaknesses, inconsistencies, etc., in professional development and initiate appropriate corrective action

- Provide your personnel an opportunity for professional and personal leadership growth

- Develop cooperative relationships among all organizational groups

- Foster leadership with global mindset--know the criticality of our global organization.

- Bottom line: develop your people to become effective leaders for the organization!

Leadership Thought Questions

- Whom are you developing with your leadership?

- How could you develop using the concepts and ideas from this book?

- What did you learn in this chapter?

- What significant ideas or points stand out in your mind?

- What ideas or points can apply to your development?

F(X) Insight

- **Lead, Follow or get the Hell Out of the Way!**

- **Leaders develop their People**

- **Leader mentor**

- **Understand what makes your people inspired and motivated**

- **Understand the relationship between feedback, dialogue and assessment**

- **All leadership is people-focused**

- **Developing your people helps to develop your team**

People-Focused Exercise

The purpose of this writing exercise is to determine what areas of growth and development you need to improve and develop in your people skills. How are your communication, relationship and empowering skills in relation to your people or team? On a separate piece of paper, or on the lines below, write down areas you feel you need to improve.

Notes

_____

_____

_____

_____

_____

_____

_____

_____

_____

_____

_____

_____

_____

F(X) Leadership Growth and Development Plan

After reading this chapter, review and reflect on the ideas and concepts presented. Think about how to integrate the ideas or concepts into one of the three growth and development areas--Personal, Professional or Leadership Competency. Think about what opportunities, challenges, resources or blind spots you may encounter when you begin your growth and development journey. Use the following questions to help you grow and develop.

1. What area will the ideas and concepts help me grow and develop?

   - Personal

   - Professional

   - Leadership

2. How will I incorporate this new talent or skill into my development?

3. What is my timeline for learning the new talent or skill?

4. What opportunity and resources exist for me to use this new talent or skill?

   - _____

   - _____

   - _____

5. What blind spots may derail me from using this new talent or skill?

   - _____

   - _____

   - _____

PART THREE

Organizational F(X)

In the southwest corner of Jackson County, Oklahoma, is a town called Altus and the home of Altus Air Force Base. When you talk about Altus, Oklahoma, you are talking about both the city and the Air Force Base. They are one. The great people of Altus, Oklahoma, have embraced the men and women of Altus Air Force Base as their own family. It is a great place to raise your family and raise future leaders in the Air Force. Altus is a place you can call home.

The Altus concept and the long-term organizational leadership strategy evolved from the "Airmen's Time" briefing Chief Master Sergeant (retired) Timmothy Dickens (Former 19th Air Force Command Chief and Senior Enlisted Advisor for Defense Information Systems Agency) presented to a team of Chief Master Sergeants (CMSgt) and Senior Master Sergeants (SMSgt) in August 2004.

Airmen's Time Acknowledgements

I had the great opportunity to work Airmen's Time and the concepts learned from the project with three Chief Master Sergeants of the Air Force (CMSAF) – CMSAF Gerald Murray, CMSAF Rodney McKinley and CMSAF James Roy. These three servant leaders understood that our enlisted Airmen are the most important assets in the Air Force and had the foresight to implement the Airmen's Time concepts.

The original members of the Strategic Leadership Team were CMSgt (retired) Robert Walker; CMSgt (retired) Raymond Brzozowski; CMSgt (retired) Demetrius Threat; CMSgt (retired) Dalton Pratt; CMSgt (retired) Errol Tummings; CMSgt (retired) Mark Ippolito; CMSgt (retired) Alfred Hicks; CMSgt (retired) Glenn Shreiner; CMSgt (retired) Luwana Hargis; CMSgt (retired) Robert Wheeler; CMSgt (retired) Brian Pickett; CMSgt (retired) James Scanlan; CMSgt (retired) Thomas Oates; CMSgt (retired) Sean Meenagh; and SMSgt (retired) Douglas Channer.

Although this organizational strategy was developed by the Senior Enlisted Leaders it would not have been as successful without the backing and full support of the Wing Commander, Vice Wing Commander, and Group Commanders, Major General (retired) Mark S. Solo; Major General Carlton D. Everhart II; Colonel (retired) Dave Miller; Major General Mark "Marshall" Dillon; Brigadier General Linda Medler; and Colonel (retired) Dawn Harl.

Other individuals that contributed, encouraged and influenced the outcome of the development of the organizational strategy and success of "Airmen's Time" were the 19th Air Force Command Chiefs. CMSgt (retired) Robert Tappana (Former 19th Air Force Command Chief); CMSgt (retired) James Suttles (Former 375th Air Wing/Command Chief); CMSgt (retired) Jeff Bowes (14th Fighter Training Wing/CCC); and CMSgt (retired) Don Schroeder (Former Vice Commandant, College Enlisted Professional Military Education).

Chapter 8

Airmen's Time: The Altus Concept

> **Key Leadership Concept**: Effective leadership begins at the top and permeates throughout the organization at all levels. This is a crucial factor in assuring that leadership is an organization-wide capability. Leaders at every level in an organization must accept the responsibility to lead, take ownership of their part of the mission and develop their people. The impact of successful leadership cascades across all departments in an organization and can affect the morale of each person. Leaders are linked to organizational culture and organizational effectiveness. Leaders who develop their people guarantee organization success.

The year 1775 was a year of great change and great emerging leadership. It was a time when the New World ideas were clashing with Old World concepts. It was a time when the common person was tired of being ruled by monarchs, dictators and tyrants. It was a time of great sacrifice and great service to the revolutionary struggle for freedom. America was forged in 1776 because great leaders emerged from the fabric of this new country and committed themselves to be free and changed history forever in the name of liberty and in the name of independence.

Winds of Change

Great frontline leaders like George Washington, John Adams, Samuel Adams, Thomas Jefferson, Benjamin Franklin, Nathaniel Greene, Alexander Hamilton, Thomas Paine and Patrick Henry. Throughout the course of history, new frontline leaders emerged each time America was in great change or in crisis. The emergence of these leaders was a testament to the lasting leadership legacy the founding fathers built. Abraham Lincoln was one of those frontline leaders that stood up during great crisis.

Lincoln was faced with a great Civil War and the dissolution of the Republic. He knew that the old ways of thinking and old concepts were not going to save the Union. He needed new ideas and new ways in order to preserve the Union. In his address to Congress on 1 December 1862, he stated:

> The dogmas of the quiet past are inadequate to the stormy present. The occasion is piled high with difficulty, and we must rise with the occasion. As our case is new, so we must think anew and act anew. We must disenthrall ourselves, and then we shall save our country.

The most significant contribution we can make as leaders today is to leave a legacy of leaders.

Thinking Anew

The original Air Force Airmen's Time concept was designed to look at the feasibility of transforming the Army's Soldier's Time training into a useable and deliverable concept for implementation by the U.S. Air Force with primary focus on the First Line Supervisor. Chief Master Sergeant of the Air Force Gerald Murray created a working group with representatives from each Major Command, Direct Reporting Unit and Forward Operating Agency to look at the feasibility and value of the concept, if the concept was deliverable for Air Force-wide implementation and to determine if similar programs or information already existed.

The Airmen's Time Working Group initially met in October 2004 at the Senior Non-Commissioned Officer Academy at Maxwell Air Force Base and continued through dialogue via electronic mail. Each working group member provided input and recommendation to Chief Master Sergeant of the Air Force Gerald Murray in mid-May 2005. Airmen's Time had four main conceptual tenets:

1) It was a "Back to Basics" leadership coupled with 21st Century technology, providing additional tools for the specific purpose of Airman Development at all levels.

2) It was also about managing "TIME" even more effectively and efficiently by more consistent interaction between supervisors and their subordinates.

3) Airmen's Time valued the input of Airmen at all levels, ensuring there was constant dialogue in how we prepare others and ourselves for the challenges we continue to face in an ever-evolving Expeditionary Air Force.

4) And finally, a concept whereby the Air Force is committed to ensuring you have the best resources, training and professional development which will enhance your capabilities as a Combat Capable Warrior.

Roles and Responsibilities

Airmen's Time also defined the roles and responsibilities for Commanders, Chiefs, Senior Non-Commissioned Officers and First Line supervisors.

1) Commanders would provide the time and resources necessary to ensure all members of their organization were trained and capable to support a lighter, leaner, more lethal Expeditionary Air Force.

2) Chiefs would monitor and provide detailed guidance for training, provide leadership expertise, check training to ensure standards were established and maintained and provide feedback to the commanders.

3) Senior Non-Commissioned Officers would protect the program against distractions and provide leadership and guidance as necessary to the First Line Supervisor.

4) First Line Supervisors would provide the best examples of supervision and leadership to their subordinates while ensuring they were technically proficient, personally/professionally developed and combat capable.

An integral part of Airmen's Time was dedicated training time conducted at least once a month for a minimum of three hours with First Line Supervisors acting as the primary trainer when possible.

Airmen's Time & Force Development Training subjects were to be in any of four areas,

1) Technical and Operational Competence

2) Expeditionary and Ancillary Skills

3) Personal and Professional Development

4) Headquarters Air Force, Major Command, Installation and Special Interest Items

The Altus Concept

The unique significance of Airmen's Time at Altus Air Force Base was the convergence of two emerging developmental concepts -- Airmen's Time and Enlisted Force Development. It combined the opportunity to teach, coach and mentor every month and to propose a model of integrated leadership development in order to grow Airmen into future Wingmen, Leaders and Warriors for the Air Force.

By developing leaders in a deliberate process, it guarantees the requisite leadership for the future. The Altus Concept had a unique caveat to the process. The whole organization would grow collectively as leaders but the individual leader was personally responsible for their development outside of the classroom. Those individuals with initiative and drive who took ownership for their continued development grew faster than those that did not.

> *"High Touch & Low Tech"*
>
> *CMSAF Bob Gaylor*

Force Development

Leadership development in the Air Force is part of the overall concept of force development. Force development is a function of both individual and Air Force institutional responsibility.

> Force development provides a leadership focus at all levels of an Airman's career through an iterative process of development involving education and training, seasoned with experience and ongoing mentoring by more experienced Airmen (AFDD 1-1, 2008, p.34).

The overall goal of force development is to link the Airman's perspective with defined competencies and processes to prepare Airmen to successfully lead and act in the midst of rapidly evolving requirements, while meeting both their personal and professional expectations.

The Air Force deliberately develops its leaders through a phased approach to create leaders in a systematic, organized manner best configured to meet the needs of the Service. There are three levels of leadership in the force development model—tactical, operational and strategic levels. A phased force development approach to leadership at the tactical, operational and strategic levels provides the framework for focusing development of institutional competencies supported by occupational skill sets. Force development is the method the Air Force uses to grow experienced, inspirational leaders who have the necessary technical competencies and professional values, framed by a common culture, regardless of career specialty. (AFDD 1-1, 2008, p. 38)

Tactical Expertise

Tactical, Operational, & Strategic Leaders

At the tactical expertise level, Airmen work to master their primary duty skills, develop competence and experience in applying those skills and begin to acquire the understanding and knowledge that will produce the qualities essential to effective leadership. Tactical leaders are the Air Force's technicians and specialists. Air Force Doctrine describes this level as primarily a leadership growth stage:

> At this level, Airmen learn about themselves as leaders and how their leadership acumen can affect others. They are focused on honing followership abilities, influencing peers, and motivating subordinates. They are learning about themselves and their impact on others in roles as both follower and leader. (AFDD 1-1, 2008, p. 39)

Operational Expertise

At the operational competence level, Airmen begin to understand the context of the larger Air Force mission. The leader also begins to understand how to lead and integrate diversity in order to accomplish the mission. This level is where an Air Force member transitions from being a specialist to understanding Air Force operational capabilities. Air Force Doctrine describes this level as the level where tactical expertise and operational competence are employed in new leadership opportunities to affect an entire theater or joint operations area.

> Based on a thorough understanding of themselves as leaders and followers and how they influence others, they apply an understanding of organizational and team dynamics. They continue to develop personal leadership skills, while developing familiarity in institutional competencies." (AFDD 1-1, 2008, p. 40)

Strategic Expertise

At the strategic vision level, Airmen combine highly developed occupational skills and institutional competencies to apply broad professional leadership capabilities. They develop a deep understanding of Air Force missions and operational capabilities. Air Force doctrine once again describes this level of leadership development as a continuing growth stage:

> They also understand how the Air Force operates within joint, multinational, and interagency relationships. At this level, an Airman has required competencies transition from the integration of people with missions to leading and directing exceptionally complex and multi-tiered organizations. Based on a thorough understanding of themselves as leaders and followers, and how to use organizational and team dynamics, they apply an in-depth understanding of leadership at the institutional and interagency levels. (AFDD 1-1, 2008, p. 41)

All three of these areas were key components of the Altus Concept.

> *Airmen's Time*
> *&*
> *Force Development*

Starting the Journey

I was living in Germany when the announcement of my selection to be the next 97th Air Mobility Wing Command Chief was released. At the time of the announcement, I was working on force development programs for the communications and computer career field.

Force development was a program of how to develop and sustain a work force through a lifecycle from Basic Military Training to retirement. It was a holistic view of training and development spanning a 30-year career with a look at how career development and professional development fit into the lifecycle of the individual and the organization.

Force development also identified some serious time gaps in our professional growth and development in comparison to career development. As I left Ramstein Air Base, Germany, for Oklahoma, I took the knowledge of force development with me.

My passion for developing leaders was fueled very early in my career by great leaders who encouraged, molded and inspired me to achieve more than I thought I could. They invested time and guided me through a solid plan of leadership development that helped to hone and build my leadership ability.

They also ensured that I had the training that refined my technical skills and provided challenges and opportunities that built my experience, which taught me lessons that development and training could not. However, they also made me responsible and accountable for my growth and development. I was responsible to grow as a leader, no one else, me.

Altus Air Force Base

When I arrived at Altus Air Force Base in June 2004, it was time to start paying back and paying forward the leadership lessons that others had invested in me. After arriving at Altus Air Force Base, I did the most important thing a leader can do--listen and observe before making changes.

Why is this important? Remember, you are the new leader and an outsider to the current organization. You have not earned the trust and respect of the organization yet. You are being looked at and assessed based on your actions and words. So choosing the right actions and words will help build the trust–respect relationship and help build your credibility as a leader to the new organization.

I spent the first 60 days learning about the organization and its organizational culture. My first stop was with my boss. I needed to understand his vision and focus for the wing, understand his concerns and his vision of my roles and responsibilities.

Second priority was to meet with each group commander, squadron commander, staff directors and senior enlisted leaders to understand their issues, challenges and focus from their perspective.

Third priority was dedicated time between visits to learn the mission, vision, goals, priorities and commander's intent to understand the culture and focus of the wing.

And finally, I visited and spent time with the First Sergeants Council, Chief's Group, the enlisted professional organizations, the Wing Career Assistance Advisor, First Term Airmen Center and the Airmen's Leadership School, getting a sense of the morale and identifying who my key enlisted leaders were in the wing. After 60 days, I had a good idea of how the wing was conducting business.

Initial Assessment

My initial assessment was that squadrons were building technically competent Airmen and had built solid working relationships within each squadron and in each group, but they were lacking wing-wide enlisted structure or a leadership-centric culture.

After the first enlisted call, it was evident that less than 30 percent knew what their responsibilities were in accordance with Air Force Instruction 36-2618, *The Enlisted Force Structure,* which defines the roles and responsibilities of each grade in the Air Force.

In order to understand the issues and assess further where we were as an enlisted force, I pulled together a core leadership team. The team consisted of the Operations Group Superintendent, Chief Master Sergeant Ray Brzozowski; Mission Support Group Superintendent, Chief Master Sergeant Rob Walker; and Wing Career Assistance Advisor, Senior Master Sergeant Sean Meenagh.

The core team did a deep dive to discover and analyze the problems and issues. We used a SWOT (strengths, weaknesses, opportunities and threats) analysis to assess the wing. We spent another 30 days identifying problems and concerns in three major areas:

1) Identifiable gaps in the professional and leadership development of wing-enlisted personnel

2) A lack of retention and use of the lessons taught during Professional Military Education, which diminished rapidly after one year

3) Deficiencies in deployment readiness training for those heading into a combat zone

From the deep dive, it became apparent that we needed to develop a way to fix the enlisted issues and knew it was our responsibility to reinforce the culture of Airmen. We decided to develop a persistent Airmen Development program at the wing that reinforced the lessons taught at Professional Military Education (PME), teach leadership development and invest in a Deployment Readiness program to answer the concerns of our deploying Airmen.

In order to tackle the problems we needed to build a strategic leadership team to tackle the issues and answer the following questions:

- What did we want as the outcomes/mindset of our Airmen Development program to have?
- How do I prepare emerging and enduring leaders for the fog and friction of war in a volatile, uncertain, complex and ambiguous (VUCA) environment and understand that tactical actions have strategic impact?

- How do I prepare emerging and enduring leaders to work with multinational partners culturally, holistically and politically?
- How do I train emerging and enduring leaders to understand that they are responsible and accountable for their actions as a leader?
- How do I train emerging and enduring leaders to understand the "new normal"?

These were the questions and concerns that the leaders at Altus Air Force Base were concerned with and struggled to develop as part of the Altus Concept. Our end-state vision at Altus Air Force Base was to produce Airmen who were better than when they and ready to face the challenges of a VUCA environment.

An Airman whose very core is infused with the Air Force core values, Air Force Core Competencies and Air Force Enduring Leadership Competencies, understands Air Force Instruction 36-2618, Air Force Doctrine Document 1-1 and Air Force Manual 10-100

It was through a leadership-centric culture of training and development that focused on leadership development, collaborative teamwork and continuous growth. We focused our training and development on emerging and enduring leaders to have the ability to survive and operate in a VUCA environment throughout their leadership career. We invested our time and energy to ensuring that emerging and enduring leaders were prepared for the future, but also to ensure we had a solid leadership bench so the organization was ready for the future.

The Plan

After 90 days in the wing I presented the concerns of the Senior Enlisted to the Wing Commander, followed by the vision and plan to combat these concerns. Our overall leadership development strategy started with a fundamental organizational philosophy of a disciplined approach to talent management and leadership development.

The strategy clearly laid out the expectations and responsibilities we had for our Airmen and their development. It also established what we, as an organization, expected in return, in regards to performance standards and expectations. The leadership development strategy also assessed the strengths, weaknesses, threats and opportunities for each individual and the leadership requirements of the organization.

Persistent Leadership & Force Development

With the Commander's approval, the Airmen's Time: The Altus Concept was implemented over an 18-month period and was divided into three operational phases:

Phase 1: Establish an enlisted force development council consisting of the Wing Command Chief, Wing Career Assistance Advisor, Group Superintendents and Wing Chief Master Sergeants

Phase 2: Define operating environment, leadership skills and migration strategies for the following:

- Develop Battlefield Deployment Training (BDT)

- Leadership Development

- Enlisted Professional Development (EPD)

- Develop a list of leadership skills necessary for each grade (AFI 36-2618)

- Develop an Enlisted Professional Development Course Schedule

- Identify necessary skills needed for EPD teaching

- Develop strategies necessary to achieve Enlisted Leadership and EPD milestones

Phase 3: Implement the Migration Strategy for Battlefield Deployment Training, Enlisted Leadership and Enlisted Professional Development

Summary

Our deliberate organizational strategy developed a persistent long-term learning process for our Airmen as they increasingly face a world where change is constant, and the battle space is increasingly volatile, uncertain, complex and ambiguous.

Thus began the leadership journey of a long-term, focused organizational strategy of investing in our Airmen by leveraging our skills, talents and experiences to transform our Airmen into future enlisted leaders.

Key Takeaways

Seek to understand the issues

A leader needs to identify and evaluate information and then use the information to effect decisions, actions and outcomes for the future.

Develop desired outcomes and strategy

Leadership outcomes and developmental strategies must be aligned with the Organization's mission, vision, core values, goals and strategic plan in order to be successful.

Analyze and use foresight

Critically analyze outcomes and strategy to understand the second, third and fourth order of effects of proposed policies or actions.

Leadership Application

The following are 10 strategies for new leaders:

- Understand the mission, vision, core values, goals and strategic plan of the new organization
- Understand the leadership environment before you act
- Be visible and accessible
- Get out and meet the people so you can find the issues
- Define the leadership reality for your organization
- Listen, observe and then listen again
- Discover the strengths, weaknesses, threats and opportunities early
- Set and reinforce the organization's standards
- Identify your future leaders and prepare them for tomorrow's challenges
- Discover who your key leaders are and start building a relationship

Leadership Thought Questions

- What is the strategic vision of the organization?
- What is the mission of the organization?
- What are the organization's primary goals, priorities and objectives?
- What are driving needs and challenges?
- What is your most critical and pressing concern right now?

F(X) Insight

- As the new leader, listen and observe before you make changes
- Talk to other leaders to discover what the issues are
- Use a broad base of information sources
- Gather information and understand the facts of the issues before you tackle the problem
- Get the right people on your side early
- Once you know the issues, create an effective leadership team to resolve the problems

S.W.O.T Exercise

The purpose of this writing exercise is to analyze your organization using the Strengths, Weaknesses, Opportunities and Threats model. Using the model below write on a separate piece of paper and analyze your work center or organization.

The SWOT analysis should give you a good starting point to see where you can help the organization achieve its goals and mission.

Strengths
- What does our organization do well?
- What talents, skills, competencies and knowledge do we have already?

Weaknesses
- What do we need to improve?
- What talents, skills, competencies and knowledge do we need to improve or develop?

Opportunities
- What are the organizational opportunities this year?
- What leadership opportunities are there this year?

Threats
- What threats will cause the organization trouble this year?

F(X) Leadership Growth and Development Plan

After reading this chapter, review and reflect on the ideas and concepts presented. Think about how to integrate the ideas or concepts into one of the three growth and development areas--Personal, Professional or Leadership Competency. Think about what opportunities, challenges, resources or blind spots you may encounter when you begin your growth and development journey. Use the following questions to help you grow and develop.

1. What area will the ideas and concepts help me grow and develop?

   - Personal

   - Professional

   - Leadership

2. How will I incorporate this new talent or skill into my development?

3. What is my timeline for learning the new talent or skill?

4. What opportunity and resources exist for me to use this new talent or skill?

   - _____

   - _____

   - _____

5. What blind spots may derail me from using this new talent or skill?

   - _____

   - _____

   - _____

Chapter 9

Collaborative Teamwork

> **Key Leadership Concept:** A team is capable of accomplishing things that no individual person, no matter how talented and gifted they are, can do alone. The strength of the team is the individual capabilities and abilities forged into one cohesive organization. A well-functioning team is committed to a common purpose and a common vision.

The day was brutally cold and the wind was raw as the soldiers marched into Valley Forge. The soldiers were fatigued and spent. As they trudged through the snow, they passed a quiet and solemn General George Washington mounted on his horse. What they could not see behind the face of their leader was the anguish of seeing his men in this condition. Many of his soldiers had just cloth wrapped around their feet instead of shoes.

Valley Forge

Blood from their bruised and ragged feet stained the snow as they walked into their winter camp. Besides his concern for resupplying the soldiers with new clothes and new shoes, his greatest concern was how to restore the spirit of the Continental Army. He knew his men were disheartened and in deep despair but not broken. As the soldiers walked underneath his gaze, they looked toward General Washington to rekindle and restore their faith in the cause of Freedom and Independence.

Courage and Hope

The story of Valley Forge is a symbol of American hope and courage and a historical turning point of the Continental Army under George Washington's leadership. During the long winter encampment, 12,000 soldiers struggled through a cold, snowy winter and severe shortages of food and clothing. No battles were fought at Valley Forge, but nearly one in four (3,000) men died in the six months from typhoid, typhus, dysentery and pneumonia.

It was a testament to General Washington's character, his ability to build a great leadership team and his ability to develop his troops. General Washington led from the front with courageous leadership and by doing so inspired his troops to greatness during that long winter.

First, he displayed his character of integrity by sharing the soldier's pain by eating only fire cakes and sleeping in a tent just like his troops. Every morning he would rise early and travel to each regiment campsite to talk and to encourage the troops. He addressed the important issues of his troops by providing food, shelter and later, adequate clothing.

Second, he assembled and developed a leadership team to help him through this struggle. Under his command were the Marquis de Lafayette, Baron Friedrich von Stueben, Alexander Hamilton (First Secretary of the Treasury), James Monroe (Fifth President of the U.S.), John Marshall (Chief Justice of the Supreme Court), Henry Knox (First Secretary of War) and Nathaniel Greene (Quartermaster of the Continental Army).

These great men helped to share the burden of taking care of the troops and provided feedback to Washington on the morale of the troops.

Last, the Continental Army was comprised of experienced fighters, but lacked the discipline and training in order to stand up against the powerful British Regulars. Under the tempered discipline, drilling and training of General Friedrich von Stueben, the Continental Army was tempered and forged from raw steel into carbon-tempered steel ready to battle. On June 19, 1778, the Continental Army marched out of Valley Forge reborn through a process of courageous leadership, perseverance, self-sacrifice and teamwork.

Collaborative Team Architect

As a collaborative team architect, General George Washington exhibited the F(X) leadership competency of Build Relationships and Alliances in Valley Forge. He understood that the relationship of the leader and the subordinate in a team relationship is built on trust, respect and dignity. Washington used his leadership influence positively and skillfully to begin action in the camp and to influence decisions and acquire necessary resources. He demonstrated the ability to build relationships and alliances across organizational functions to accomplish common goals.

Washington enlarged and empowered all team members to work collaboratively and collectively within and across functions. He was culturally smart and talented and used his cultural awareness to lead across barriers and generations and understood how to work with people of different countries and cultures. Finally, he used Baron Von Steuben to provide needed guidance and development to become a truly great team.

Organizations today need the same kind of leadership, teamwork and development from their leaders that General Washington gave to his troops at Valley Forge. People need leaders who know their potential, even when they do not see it themselves, to forge them into a collaborative team.

Developing the Team

The Enlisted Force Development Council (EFDC) began as a loosely organized and underdeveloped core of dedicated Senior Non-Commissioned Officers (SNCOs) who realized the need, from their own development and experience, for better leadership and skills development at the tactical and operational level.

This team transformed into an effective and efficient team with a collective view that strengthened and developed the enlisted force by working together toward a common goal of cross-functional Airmen Development across all groups and squadrons in the wing.

However, what we did not expect or plan for was the emergent organizational strategy that formed as the EFDC developed into an influential strategic leadership force. This strategic leadership team influenced changes throughout the wing, other Air Force Bases and finally the enlisted developmental continuum for the Air Force Enlisted Professional Development.

Team Development

Each member of the EFDC completed a Multifactor Leadership Questionnaire, Learning Tactics Inventory, DISC assessment, a Myers Briggs Type Indicator assessment and attended a John Maxwell *21 Irrefutable Laws of Leadership* seminar. In addition, each member completed the John Maxwell *360 Degree Leadership* workshop and received a 360 Leader profile from the Maxwell organization. This strategic development helped each member understand what his or her leadership styles were and allowed for greater understanding of what we were embarking on with Airmen's Time.

Transformational Teamwork

Transformational leadership is a way of leading in which the leader is a coach, a mentor and a teacher. The leader is not only concerned with improving conditions within existing frameworks and mindsets, but with going one step further to design and lead processes that shift the frameworks and mindsets themselves.

Transformational leadership involves developing individuals by tapping into their sources of inspiration, innovation, creativity and drive to create a better future and is critical for the development of individuals and organizations.

The EFDC used the concept of transformational leadership in our approach to leading the Airmen, in our role as the "Enlisted Force Development Change Agent" in the wing and as the role model for the enlisted force. We sought to inspire trust, increase self-confidence, a sense of higher purpose and to build a leadership-centric legacy the Airmen could emulate.

James Kouzes and Barry Posner in their book, *A Leader's Legacy*, encapsulate the actual intent and vision of the strategic leadership team from the start of Airmen's Time. "Exemplary leaders are interested more in others success than in their own" (Kouzes and Posner, 2006, p.10) which is the definition of Service Before Self.

The one common theme for the EFDC was--as Senior Non-Commissioned Officers, we are to lead from the front, take care of Airmen, and serve as role models, in accordance with Air Force Instruction 36-2618, Chapter 5, paragraph 5.1.3:

> Be an active, visible leader. Develop their NCOs into better leaders and supervisors. Deliberately grow and prepare their NCOs to be effective future Senior Non-Commissioned Officers.

The EFDC reinforced the Air Force Doctrine Directive 1-1 goals and the concepts taught at Professional Military Education. Air Force Doctrine Directive 1-1 (AFDD 1-1) was the leadership vision of Airmen's Time.

> Leadership is fundamental to the United States Air Force. Creating future Air Force leaders is the responsibility of the current leaders, and force development is their tool to do so. The more effort placed in using this tool, the better the leaders it will produce. By using the organized approach of developing leaders from the tactical level, through the operational, leading to the most senior strategic levels in the Air Force, the Service will ensure its continued preeminent position in the world. Leaders are

inextricably linked to mission effectiveness; developing those leaders in a deliberate process that guarantees the Air Force will produce the requisite leadership. Leadership and force development must continue to provide the Air Force with its most valuable resource: its people, its motivated and superbly qualified Airmen. (p. 20)

The Air Force Core Competency of Developing Airmen was the mission of Airmen's Time.

The ultimate source of combat capability resides in the men and women of the Air Force. The full-spectrum capabilities of our Service stem from the collective abilities of our Total Force; the abilities of our people stem from a career-long focus on the development of professional Airmen. (Air Force Posture Statement, 2006, p. 27)

Collaborative Team

The EFDC used a front-end analysis and a needs analysis to design and develop our leadership development program. The front-end analysis served as the foundation of our program development and helped to establish the necessary benchmarks for the success of the program. The needs analysis helped to define the core needs and helped to define our integrated leadership development strategy.

The EFDC fused enlisted professional development, enlisted leadership development, mentoring, AFSC skills development and battlefield deployment training into a deliberate organizational strategy to strengthen and improve the Airmen. This training focused on persistent professional development throughout the career from first term Airmen to retirement.

The research conducted in developing our strategy defined the operating environment, necessary skills and wing migration strategy of the enlisted force development annually. This strategy produced a tri-track development concept plan versus a traditional dual-track plan. The incorporation of the third track, "Warrior Skills", brought the importance of the necessary skills to survive and operate in a VUCA environment.

Charter

A charter was developed by the EFDC which established the purpose, goals, mission and duties. The implementation strategy required us to broaden the scope of professional development and to inspire continuous self-improvement through educational and developmental opportunities. It required us to focus on attention to detail, discipline and dedication to the highest principles and standards that define all activities surrounding the wing's missions and required us to be hands-on leaders. The overall key strategic drivers for the deliberate organizational strategy were:

- Fostering leadership with a warrior mindset--knowing the criticality of our global mission and the impact we have both on the fight we are in and the fight we deter

- Focus on the critical role leadership plays in executing the wing's missions

- Highlight important attributes, traits or aspects of leadership and leaders

- Create opportunities to improve individual leadership capacity and capability

- Implement or improve programs designed to develop leaders

- Encourage and facilitate—leadership encounters between leaders and their troops

- Evaluate enlisted professional development and training to determine if the changes improve the enlisted force and are consistent with the Service direction

- Identifying opportunities for improvement, as well as problems, weaknesses and inconsistencies in professional development and initiate appropriate corrective action

- Display a sincere interest in subordinates career development and career progression

- Provide personnel an opportunity for professional and personal leadership growth

- Develop cooperative relationships and teamwork among all enlisted groups

- Provide commanders with dedicated, motivated battle-ready warriors

- **Bottom line**: Develop followers to become effective leaders

Our development plan established a roadmap of assessment, development and feedback that each Airman and organization could refer to for success in an uncertain future.

Program Development

When developing a leadership development program it is key and essential to organize the program around the organization's mission, vision and core values. Remember you are building leaders for the organization's future so they must be representative of the organization's mission, vision and core values.

By developing your program around these three areas will ensure you meet the intent of the organization's overall business strategy and outlook. The program needs to be a long-term focused organizational strategy of investing in your people by developing their skills, talents and experiences to transform them into future organizational leaders.

Invest in Everyone

You need to develop everyone in the organization but not equally. Why? Not everyone in your organization is at the same level of personal maturity, leadership maturity or educational readiness to be developed equally.

Each person in your organization is a emerging leader, enduring leader or an experienced leader so they must be developed based on where they are in their development.

Avoid the cookie cutter approach or the "one size fits all" approach when developing your people. Establish individualized learning plans for all participants based on individualized assessment.

By developing each person at their level of readiness will ensure that people are developed at their level of competence and ensure that the leadership pipeline always has bench strength of developing leaders for the organization.

Build Mentors

You need to equip your senior leaders to be teachers, coaches and mentors for the potential and emerging leaders. You have invested a great deal of capital in their development so it is time they give back to the organization to help it grow the next generation of leaders.

Outcome Based Program

Your leadership development program needs to be outcome-based and provide senior leadership a way to measure the return on investment. This will provide your organization with a way to measure how well the program is developing its leaders and measures up to the organization's mission, vision and core values. It will also focus your development around what is critical and important to the organization and provide direction for future growth

Multi-Discipline Approach

Your leadership development program should use a multi-discipline approach to development. Since most leadership development is done in classrooms, seminars, webinars and through computer-based learning, you need to provide opportunities to apply the learned skills.

This can be done by assigning people to tiger teams, advisory boards and working groups or lead project officers for business events (i.e. picnics, banquets, or community outreach programs).

Leadership Centric Culture

Finally, your leadership development program should create a leadership-centered culture that contributes to a foundation of trust and mutual respect, which drives greater mission success. Another important aspect of leadership development is creating and sustaining an organizational culture conducive to learning and development so that leadership can flourish and prosper.

Summary

A leader understands that a good team needs guidance and development to become a truly great team. They demonstrate the ability to build relationships and alliances across organizational functions to accomplish common goals. Your people deserve not only the best resources but also the best leadership you can provide them. You must set them up for success.

Notes

_____

_____

_____

_____

Key Takeaways

Seek to inspire trust and a higher sense of purpose

Trust is essential to leadership. No one wants to follow an untrustworthy leader. Trust means you are true to your word and you are an authentic leader.

Promote positive teamwork

Positive teamwork supports the organization's goals and objectives and fosters behavior directed toward the achievement of theses ends. Teamwork that supports hard work, loyalty, quality consciousness or concern for customer satisfaction are examples of positive norms.

A team accomplishes more than an individual

A team is capable of accomplishing things that no individual person, no matter how talented and gifted they are, can do alone.

Leadership Application

The following are 10 strategies for building a better team:

- Create a team identity
- Clarify the team's mission
- Create and maintain a win-win atmosphere
- Establish a charter to define your team goals and objectives
- Develop and grow your team daily
- Motivate and inspire your team to internalize organizational goals, vision and core values
- Take time to develop collaborative relationships
- Invest in relationship building exercises
- Invest in strategic team development, testing and assessments to help define your team make-up
- Establish clear lines of communication, feedback and dialogue

Leadership Thought Questions

- Do you have a team charter?

- What are the goals of your team?

- How do you develop and grow your team?

- What is your team development strategy?

- Do you know the skills and talents of your team?

- How are strategic teams developed in your organization?

- Are your team members passionate about leading in the organization?

F(X) Insight

- Once you know where you are going, make a plan to achieve the goals

- Communicate team goals, priorities or expectations

- Involve everyone in the change

- Establish a charter with enough detail that everyone understands the vision and goals

- Lead by example and set the tone for change

- Recognize and celebrate team accomplishments

TEAM Charter Exercise

The purpose of this writing exercise is to write a team charter defining the roles and responsibilities of your team. On a separate piece of paper, or on the lines below, write down the roles and responsibilities of your team and what you plan to accomplish. What is the purpose of the team, what are the goals and what legacy do you want to leave.

The charter should clearly state how the team's tasks and outcomes would help the organization achieve its goals and ensure mission accomplishment.

Notes

_____

_____

_____

_____

_____

_____

_____

_____

_____

F(X) Leadership Growth and Development Plan

After reading this chapter, review and reflect on the ideas and concepts presented. Think about how to integrate the ideas or concepts into one of the three growth and development areas--Personal, Professional or Leadership Competency. Think about what opportunities, challenges, resources or blind spots you may encounter when you begin your growth and development journey. Use the following questions to help you grow and develop.

1. What area will the ideas and concepts help me grow and develop?

    - Personal

    - Professional

    - Leadership

2. How will I incorporate this new talent or skill into my development?

3. What is my timeline for learning the new talent or skill?

4. What opportunity and resources exist for me to use this new talent or skill?

    - _____

    - _____

    - _____

5. What blind spots may derail me from using this new talent or skill?

    - _____

    - _____

    - _____

Chapter 10

Leadership Models

> **Key Leadership Concept**: Leadership and leadership development is critical to military success in peacetime and war. Identifying, developing and preparing future leaders is the ultimate goal of professional military education, professional development and is a key responsibility of every leader.

S trategically leading your human capital to their maximum potential and developing the necessary social capital can help you create dynamic teams to meet the challenges of the future. Airmen's Time utilized the F(X) models and the Inspire or Retire Theorem for the development of the enlisted force.

The Altus Concept was a hands-on leader engagement with our people. It required both leader and follower accountability and responsibility to make it work. The Altus Concept was a way of thinking about the development of the individual leader, the collective development of all leaders and the overall impact it would have on the organization.

Inspire or Retire

The Inspire or Retire Theorem, which was discussed earlier in the book, was the first part of the Altus Concept. It was a declaration to all the SNCOs in the wing to live up to the high standards and principles of Air Force leadership. It was EFDCs motto and way of telling each SNCO that you needed to heed the battle cry or seek new employment.

Those SNCOs who did not want to change or resisted the push for development, we asked to retire. This may sound harsh, but we had a responsibility to the Country and the Air Force to train and equip our greatest national treasure--the next generation of Airmen and attitudes of "it's all about me" are a poison to our Airmen. Growth sometimes requires sacrifice for the greater good of the organization. The theorem was a visual representation of our expectations of senior enlisted leadership, our organizational vision, goals, and values and the impact we could make on our people.

The theorem was the expectation of all leaders and followers alike during Airmen's Time. The expectation was for the Non-Commissioned Officers and Senior Non-Commissioned Officers to inspire their Airmen to become better leaders. The main function is to lead People and execute the organizational mission and the final analysis would be to "Inspire or Retire."

SNCO

$$\int f^{(x)}{}_{(P+M)} \left[\frac{RE^{(LxE)} + L\,(360°) + DL^{(10X)} + R^{(TPMS)}}{(CV \times AC)} \right] + AF^{(MxVxSPxP)} = WLW^{(21C)} \quad \begin{array}{l} \text{Yes} \nearrow \text{Inspire} \\ \text{No} \searrow \text{Retire} \end{array}$$

Junior Enlisted

In addition, it was a statement of our commitment to continue to grow and develop ourselves and our people on a continuous basis.

The overall concept of the Inspire or Retire Theorem is that from the most Junior enlisted to each SNCO the function of every leader was to lead People (P) and execute the Mission (M).

The foundation of enlisted leadership is the Core Values (CV) and the Airman's Creed (AC) fused together with RE (LxE) = Responsibility to lead by example + L (360°) = 360 Leadership + DL (10X) = the concept of developing Airmen as leaders versus just followers multiplies your leadership capacity by 10 fold + R = Resiliency (Technically, Physically, Mentally, Spiritually).

After compiling the inner equation, a leader must have a complete understanding of the (M) Mission x (V) Vision x (SP) Strategic Plan x (P) Priorities of the Air Force in order to develop a 21st Century Wingman, Leader and Warrior with a desire and mindset to be amazing and to inspire our Airmen = WLW (21C).

The Inspire or Retire Theorem helped to define the mindset and culture shift we were seeking to make. The next challenge was establishing outcomes and the effects needed to achieve those outcomes.

The process of identifying outcomes and formulating a Leadership Strategy and Force Development Plan was the use of the Leadership-Based Outcomes/Mindset (LBO/M) cycle model, the Instructional Systems

Design model and the four leadership quadrants as defined in The Center of Creative Leadership's *Handbook of Leadership Development* by Cynthia D. McCauley and Ellen Van Velsor.

During this effects-producing process, our leadership development, force development and battlefield deployment strategies were determined, developmental options reviewed and Airmen's Time Development approved. Our desired outcome/mindset changes was to produce a new breed of Airmen.

Leadership-Based Outcomes/Mindset Model

The LBO/M five stage cycle process was from the briefing titled *Effects-based Operations: Change in the Nature of War,* authored by Lieutenant General David A. Deptula (Retired), and first published by the Aerospace Education Foundation in 2001.

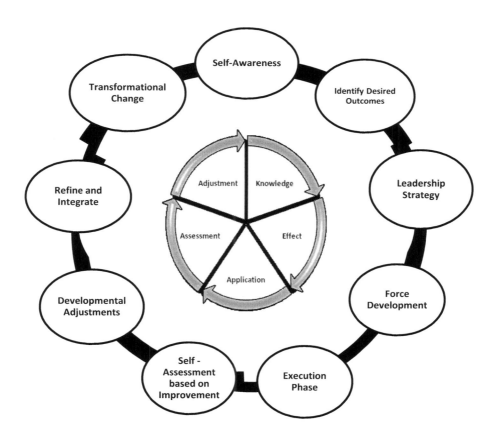

The five elements within the center consist of the following:

- Knowledge
- Effect
- Application
- Assessment
- Adjustment

Knowledge

The five-step process begins with the Knowledge stage which requires a comprehensive understanding of professional development and the leadership development environment at Altus.

Effect

The Effect stage was where the leadership strategy and force development planning occurred focused on desired future states or outcomes/mindset.

Application

The Application stage was where the actual execution of the leadership and force development and battlefield deployment training took place.

Assessment

The Assessment stage focused on the impact of the effects by collecting and analyzing results of the effects based on (Likert (1-5 Scale) surveys from participants, facilitators and Squadron Commanders).

Adjustment

The Adjustment stage is where the leadership, force development and battlefield deployment courses of action were validated and modified to produce new levels of knowledge of our professional development and leadership development strategies.

Instructional Design

Another key developmental model used was the Instructional System Design (ISD) model, which was used to build and design the leadership learning strategy. The ISD model provided the team with the who, what, where, why and how of our learning strategy and program. The ISD model has five steps of evaluation

- Analyze
- Design
- Develop
- Implement
- Evaluation

Analyze

The Analyze phase was used to determine the desired outcome, compile a task inventory, select desired tasks and choose the desired instructional setting.

Design

The Design phase developed our learning objectives, identified learning steps and developed a sequencing structure for the learning objectives.

Develop

In the Develop phase, we reviewed current courseware, developed further courseware and validated the courseware to ensure it met the objectives of Airmen's Time.

Implement

The Implement stage correlates to the Execution phase of the LBM/O Model. After the hard work of the first three phases, the actual training was conducted in the Implement phase.

Evaluation

Finally, we reviewed and evaluated the lessons taught and made adjustments to the courseware based on student and instructor feedback in the Evaluation phase.

Four Quadrants

The use of the LBM/O and the ISD were critical to implementing the final model of development. Our leadership development process categorized wing enlisted personnel in four quadrants as defined in The Center for Creative Leadership's *Handbook of Leadership Development* by Cynthia D. McCauley and Ellen Van Velsor.

Leader Development Key Stakeholders (CMSgt/SMSgt/First Sergeant) 360 Leadership Mirrors 360 John Maxwell Series Learning Tactics Inventory Wing Teachers, Mentors and Coaches	Team and Organization Development Key Stakeholders (MSgt and below) Scenario Based Development 21 Irrefutable Laws, John Maxwell Series Leadership/Followership Courses Developmental Assignments
Connection Key Stakeholders Enlisted Wing Personnel) Cross-Functional Teaming Cross-Functional Feedback Cross-Functional Networking	Developmental Assignments Key Stakeholders (Enlisted Wing Personnel) Enlisted Organizational Roles Wing-wide Impact Roles Enlisted Development Facilitators Enlisted Development Coordinators

Our Leadership development process focused on developing key stakeholders (Senior Enlisted Leaders) while continuing to develop our Team and Organizational Stakeholders (MSgt through AB).

By utilizing this multi-layered approach, we continued the growth and development of all our enlisted leaders across the wing. The developmental assignments in the third quadrant helped to build an emerging leader's leadership skills and build confidence in their abilities.

Finally, quadrant four provided the best return on investment benefit. The cross-functional communication across the wing grew exponentially because the four groups worked together every month in a combined classroom and learning environment.

As discussed earlier in this book, we followed AFDD 1-1's tactical guiding principles in order to measure our growth and impact of training against them.

Summary

A leader needs to understand the overall mission and vision of the organization while inspiring trust, increasing self-confidence, providing a sense of higher purpose and ultimately building a leadership-centric legacy that all can emulate.

With these common leadership models, all aspects of leader development were coordinated and individual progress against this model was monitored.

Our developmental thought process was that "leadership" needed to be taught to Airmen from the start of their career and reinforced at each step of their career progression.

If done correctly and with the thought in mind that the wing is in partnership with Enlisted Professional Development, then the Force Development goal of getting the right people, in the right job, at the right time, with the right skills to fight and win in support of our national security objectives, will happen.

"The Air Force needs a long-term, focused organizational strategy of investing in our Airmen by leveraging our skills, talents and experiences to transform our Airmen into future strategic leaders."

Chief Master Sergeant Thomas S. Narofsky
US Strategic Command Senior Enlisted Leader
Air Force Doctrine Document 1-1
8 November 2011

Key Takeaways

Leadership development is critical to organizational success

Today, organizational leadership is a necessity. Every person in an organization needs to be able to lead through complexity and ambiguity.

Develop a strategic plan for leadership development

Use an organized, disciplined and well-developed approach to developing your people.

Set high standards and high expectations for your leadership development program

Ensure your people understand that leadership development is not an option, it is a business necessity.

Leadership Application

The following are 10 strategies for a leadership development plan.

- Do a deep dive and discover what your organizational leadership needs truly are
- Define your leadership development objectives and outcomes
- Use a disciplined approach to your leadership development
- Define your strategy based on the desired objectives and outcomes
- Implement your strategy to produce the effects your organization needs
- Assess the impact of your leadership development plan daily
- Adjust, refine and integrate the results to improve your leadership development
- Develop all your people to build your organizational leadership bench strength
- Develop key leaders through developmental assignments to stretch and grow their capability
- Assess the return of investment and discontinue or refine actions that do not produce the necessary results

Leadership Thought Questions

- How do you develop leaders in your organization?

- What are the leadership skills your organization will need for the future?

- What can you do to help your organization develop leaders?

- How do you lead the change necessary to build a leadership development strategy?

- What kind of pushback do you expect from the need for change?

F(X) Insight

- **Take the time to invest in your organization and build your future leaders**

- **Leadership development is an organization necessity**

- **Develop your leadership pipeline and seek out your high-potential leaders**

- **Look for your late blooming leaders**

- **Build strategic alliances to further your development process**

- **Reinforce your organizational core values**

Development Plan Exercise

The purpose of this writing exercise is to define the leadership needs of your work center or organization. On a separate piece of paper or on the lines below write down what key skills, talents and mindsets your team or your organization will need to meet future challenges and opportunities. After you define the leadership requirements, develop a strategy and then a plan to develop the skills, talents and mindsets for your team or organization.

Notes

_____

_____

_____

_____

_____

_____

_____

_____

_____

_____

_____

F(X) Leadership Growth and Development Plan

After reading this chapter, review and reflect on the ideas and concepts presented. Think about how to integrate the ideas or concepts into one of the three growth and development areas--Personal, Professional or Leadership Competency. Think about what opportunities, challenges, resources or blind spots you may encounter when you begin your growth and development journey. Use the following questions to help you grow and develop.

1. What area will the ideas and concepts help me grow and develop?

   - Personal

   - Professional

   - Leadership

2. How will I incorporate this new talent or skill into my development?

3. What is my timeline for learning the new talent or skill?

4. What opportunity and resources exist for me to use this new talent or skill?

   - _____

   - _____

   - _____

5. What blind spots may derail me from using this new talent or skill?

   - _____

   - _____

   - _____

Chapter 11

Strategic Communications Plan

> **Key Leadership Concept**: The purpose of the Airmen's Time/Airmen Development communications strategy was to inform and engage wing personnel, to include senior leaders and military, civilian and contractor employees, of the scope and intent of the Airmen's Time program and to discuss the objectives.

In any endeavor, you need to plan how you spread the news about the project or program from the time it is envisioned to the time it is implemented. The EFDC developed a strategic communications plan to implement Airmen's Time and to announce the implementation of the program. Several questions developed as part of the communications strategy and brainstorming session in order to ensure we focused our communications plan correctly.

- Do people understand the purpose of the change?

- Do people understand the vision?

- Does senior leadership support the outcomes?

- Have I created an operational plan for effectively managing the program?

- Do our people not only buy-in to the program, but do they have a sense of ownership as well?

- Have I painted a strategic picture of the expected leadership outcomes and communicated them effectively?

- Have I checked to see if our communications strategy, policy and procedures are consistent with our expected outcomes?

- Have I created a new identity to embody the new culture, conduct and capability of the program?

- Have I created a sense of urgency to get people moving toward the program goals?

Communications Strategy

The communications strategy utilized transformational change management methodologies to provide personnel with clear, transparent and consistent information to support the successful implementation of Airmen's Time. Our strategic leadership strategy and detailed enlisted engagement tactical plan incorporated the following:

- Identify key change agents within each group, squadron and work center and involve them as champions for the program

- Understand Airmen's needs and aspirations and then make a concerted effort to accommodate them

- Equip leaders to drive transformational change

- Equip leaders with the unique knowledge and skills needed to make the program successful

- Use methodologies tailored to meet the plan's strategic goals and focus on three key transformational areas:

  - Strategic Leadership and Enlisted Engagement
  - Culture definition
  - Communication methods and tactics

Strategic Leader Engagement and Awareness

The EFDC gained commitment from senior leaders to communicate the overall plan to the enlisted force. It began at the very start of the program and continued until the end. This phase focused first on the command leadership targeting wing, group and squadron commanders with one-on-one meetings to gain buy-in and to increase awareness of the program.

The second part of the phase was focused on enlisted personnel. It announced the program and made sure they understood why we were implementing the Airmen's Time program and a leadership development program. It was initiated in October 2004 and continued until January 2005 with the kickoff of the programs. In the course of this phase, key messages were communicated and the following activities took place:

- Coordination of the staff package to 97th AMW/CC on the program initiatives and intent and to report the finding of the deep dive and formation of the EFDC

- Coordination of a wing commander leadership message to the wing on the implementation of Airmen's Time describing the purpose, key milestones and his full support

- Delivery of proposed key messages for command-level communications to ensure consistent messaging

- Coordination with Public Affairs for Airmen's Time and Airman Development kick-off article and follow on messages

- Enlisted Calls to reinforce the message and provide updates and to receive raw feedback

Program Execution

During program implementation and execution, several news articles and leadership messages were published to capture our early successes and to keep the enlisted force focused on the purpose and intent of the program. A comprehensive strategy and detailed tactical plan incorporated the following:

- Think high-touch, not high tech: Make a deliberate effort to connect enlisted personnel and first line supervisors to discuss Airmen's Time and why it is important

- Leadership by example: Our actions speak louder than words, so get people directly involved in the Airmen's Time program

- Establish a two-way dialogue: Collaborative communication to ensure the message was received and understood

- Be sure to deliver consistent messages to every group, both inside and outside the organization

Assessment and Adjustment

During this phase, assessment and adjustment of the programs occurred. This phase started after the first classes were started and was an iterative process. Assessment and adjustment was a continuous process of evaluation, readjustment and innovation. Each month an exit survey for each class was utilized to determine the effectiveness of the lessons taught and the effectiveness of each facilitator.

The survey was a Likert style survey with a rating scale of one for lowest and four for highest. The following criteria was utilized:

1 = The objective of this lesson was met
2 = Lesson content was adequate
3 = Length of lesson was adequate
4 = Visual aids were conducive to learning
5 = Facilitator demonstrated thorough knowledge of subject
6 = This lesson will assist me in meeting my responsibilities as outlined in AFI 36-2618

Communication Methods and Tactics

Selecting the right mechanism to deliver messages was an important aspect of the communications process. Incorporating as many communication tools as possible to deliver a consistent message increased the amount of information that was heard and remembered. The following were several ways the message was delivered:

- Printed Materials: Products, such as brochures and flyers, were used to communicate key concepts of Airmen's Time and the Airmen Development program; the materials were disseminated through the wing via the Air Force Knowledge Now website

- Website Updates: Leadership messages, up-to-date information on training opportunities, leadership opportunities, leadership resources and other leadership development links were posted on our website monthly

- Email: Delivered messages from senior leadership, who in turn cascaded messages throughout their organization

- Enlisted Calls: Ensured all enlisted personnel were aware of all issues

- Drive-by: Unstructured opportunities that provided an effective and efficient way to share best practices, maintain and enhance knowledge and encourage performance

Summary

John P. Kotter, in his book *Leading Change,* identified two areas that the Altus Concept infused into the overall strategy--Communicating the Change Vision and Anchoring New Approaches in the Culture. The development of the Strategic Communications Plan helped to communicate the vision and the outcomes of that vision. It also helped to identify the Why and How of the program. The Anchoring of New Approaches in the Culture helped to change the mindset.

Communication tells your people that you consider them a key and vital member of your team and that you trust them. The lack of communication is the reason why teams fail. A team leader needs to effectively communicate the strategic message of the organization and keep them informed of changes, upcoming events and to inspire trust and respect in the group. Your people are not mushrooms, so do not treat them like mushrooms!

Notes

_____

_____

_____

_____

_____

_____

_____

_____

_____

Key Takeaways

Communication is key to informing and engaging. people

A well-developed communications plan will eliminate ambiguity and uncertainty in change management.

Develop a strategic communications plan

Change management requires a clear and precise communications plan to ensure everyone involved in the change understands the scope and purpose for the change.

Identify your change agents

Organizational change requires champions who will influence and guide the change in each work center.

Leadership Application

The following are 10 strategies for a communications plan:

- Brainstorm and ask analytical questions to develop your communications strategy
- Use change management methodologies to guide your communications plan development
- Define your communications plan objectives and goals
- Target your plan to engage senior leaders first
- Senior Leaders are a key part of the communications plan
- Implement a broad based media campaign to inform and engage across the organization
- Develop clear and concise messages and themes to define the scope of the change
- Assess the results of the campaign
- Make adjustments to the communications plan based on assessments
- Ensure the communications strategy and campaign run through the entire change

Leadership Thought Questions

- What organizational change are you currently going through that could use a communications strategy?

- What organizational change did you go through that did not have a communications plan? How well was the change managed?

- What information do you need to share and how do you intend to communicate your ideas?

- How can you communicate effectively the change to your team or your organization?

- As a leader, how do you implement change?

- How do you ensure everyone understands the vision and culture shift?

F(X) Insight

- **Communication is vital to leadership and moving organizations forward**
- **Ambiguity can be reduced through clear and precise communication**
- **Develop your communications skill as you develop your leadership skills**
- **Clear communication helps to build solid teams and alliances**
- **A lack of communication breeds distrust among team members**
- **An inspiring vision is dead unless it is communicated**

Communications Plan Exercise

The purpose of this writing exercise is to define a communications strategy for your work center or organization. On a separate piece of paper or on the lines below write down what questions you will need to ask to define and clarify your communications plan. After you completed the questions, answer them. Once the questions are answered, define your communications plan by defining your target audience. After you define your target audience, you need to develop a strategy and then a plan to implement a communications strategy and a media campaign.

Notes

_____

_____

_____

_____

_____

_____

_____

_____

_____

_____

_____

_____

F(X) Leadership Growth and Development Plan

After reading this chapter, review and reflect on the ideas and concepts presented. Think about how to integrate the ideas or concepts into one of the three growth and development areas--Personal, Professional or Leadership Competency. Think about what opportunities, challenges, resources or blind spots you may encounter when you begin your growth and development journey. Use the following questions to help you grow and develop.

1. What area will the ideas and concepts help me grow and develop?

   - Personal

   - Professional

   - Leadership

2. How will I incorporate this new talent or skill into my development?

3. What is my timeline for learning the new talent or skill?

4. What opportunity and resources exist for me to use this new talent or skill?

   - _____

   - _____

   - _____

5. What blind spots may derail me from using this new talent or skill?

   - _____

   - _____

   - _____

Chapter 12

Culture Shift

> **Key Leadership Concept**: The impact of successful leadership cascades across all departments in an organization and can affect the morale of each person. Leaders are the linchpin to the organizations' culture and organizational effectiveness. Leaders who develop their people guarantee organizational success.

D uring Airmen's Time, we set out to reinforce the culture of Airmen and the leadership lessons taught at Professional Military Education already established by the Air Force by changing the organizational culture of how we addressed leadership development.

Culture Change

In order to change the organizational culture you need to begin with the individual. The leader sets the tone and mood of an organizations' culture and work environment. Through the leader's words and actions he lives out the culture he wants the organization to follow. When your words and actions are not congruent, then the organization will have a culture of disbelief and untrustworthiness. Behavior and culture must align with one another in order for change to happen. As a leader, you must make sure you do not live by two sets of values, one for yourself, and one for your people. Leading by example is the most important thing.

Air Force Core Values

The Air Force's core values are Integrity First, Service before Self and Excellence in All We Do. These core values are the solid foundation upon which Air Force Leadership stands on.

The first foundational core value is Integrity. Everything rests on this core value. "Integrity is the basis of trust, and trust is the unbreakable bond that unifies leaders with their followers and commanders with their units.

Trust makes leaders effective, and integrity underpins trust" (AFDD 1-1, 2006, p. iii). Without trust, there is no foundation for leadership.

The second core value is Service before Self. "Service before Self is the essence of our commitment to the nation. Leaders who serve selflessly inspire support from everyone in their command and promote a spirit that binds organizations into an effective warfighting team" (AFDD 1-1, 2006, p. iii). Finally, the last core value is Excellence in All We Do. This core value is "our commitment to the highest standards" (AFDD 1-1, 2006, p. iii).

In order to ingrain the new culture of leadership, we developed the right leadership models, engaged key stakeholders, identified key cultural drivers and established training and development to align the culture to the desired future outcome. As the culture of enlisted development took hold in the wing, we needed visual signs to represent a change in the wing culture and our high standards and high expectation for every enlisted person attached to the wing.

S.T.R.I.P.E.S

One of the key items which helped to reinforce the change was the S.T.R.I.P.E.S poster. The S.T.R.I.P.E.S acronym reinforced what we expected of all who wore stripes in the wing--Standards, Teamwork, Responsibility, Integrity, Professionalism, Excellence in All We Do and Service before Self.

- Standards – Air Force Instruction 36-2618 is the solid foundation of the stripes I wear and the standard I MUST live up to. The Chiefs in the organization ensured the standards were followed and the best way to do that was to set the example that we wanted the Airmen to follow. We needed to be the role models for the wing. We needed to live the standards and emulate the standards first.

- Teamwork – Nothing is accomplished in the Air Force by one individual…it takes a team. There are no Lone Rangers or Lone Wolf McQuades in the Air Force.

- Responsibility – I am responsible to my Country and the Air Force to take care of the greatest national treasure—the people I lead everyday. Responsibility and accountability are two key ingredients in this principle. I am responsible and I am accountable. I am responsible for the training, coaching, mentoring and developing of the next generation of the Air Force. And, I am accountable to my Country and the Air Force to make sure that they are ready for whenever they are called upon.

- Integrity First – Foundation of Trust and Respect in everything I do! Trust is a vital leadership asset. The little "blue book" that defines trust and trustworthiness for an Air Force Leader. It is the Core Value of Integrity First. Integrity is a character trait. It is the willingness to do what is right even when no one is looking. It is the "moral compass"—the inner voice; the voice of self–control;

the basis for the trust imperative in today's military. A leader should be Omni-Integerus— Integrity, first, last and always. People need leaders with ever-present integrity at the very core of their character. Without integrity, there is no trust in your leadership, no confidence in your actions and your words have no meaning.

- Professionalism – I am a part of the Profession of Arms and I am a Professional Warrior. Understanding that you are a part of the Profession of Arms is vital for every Airman to understand. When we entered the Air Force, we took the Oath of enlistment. "I, _____, do solemnly swear (or affirm) that I will support and defend the Constitution of the United States against all enemies, foreign and domestic; that I will bear true faith and allegiance to the same; and that I will obey the orders of the President of the United States and the orders of the officers appointed over me, according to regulations and the Uniform Code of Military Justice. So help me God." Airmen join for many reasons. They join for the benefits or for school or to get out of a bad situation but they need to understand that they join to serve their Nation and may give their life in its defense.

- Excellence in All We Do – 100% of my effort and myself—nothing less will do. People need leaders who are Omni-Excellantus—always seeking excellence in all we do. Leaders who see a person's potential even when they do not see it themselves and leaders who strive for excellence in themselves and their team.

- Service before Self – it is not about me...it is about my Country, the Air Force and the People I serve. They need Leaders who are Omni-Servantus--Service before self, Always. People need a leader who serves because it is an honor and privilege. It is not about you, never has been, never will be, it is about service before self, it is about service to America, the Air Force and the people you serve by wearing this Uniform.

Another key culture change message was the Warrior Triad of Leadership, Teamwork and Growth. This change message connected the present with the past. It was built from the wing patch, tail flash of the 97th Air Mobility Wing and represents the great heritage of the 97th Bombardment Group.

Signs of Progress

The "Flaming Spear" has been the Mighty 97th Wing emblem for over 60 years. The motto: Venit Hora is Latin for "The HOUR has COME." We used this connection to the past to identify with the great leaders of the wing and to signify the HOUR had COME for enlisted leadership development. Finally, we let everyone know that a culture shift was happening at Altus Air Force Base. We put it on the entrance sign to the base.

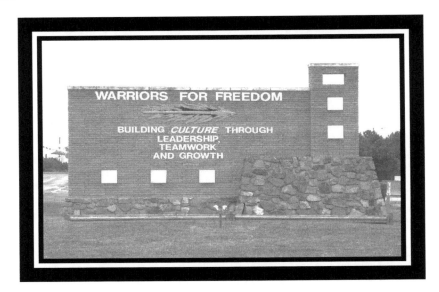

Summary

By understanding and creating an effective organizational culture you can unleash the full potential of your leadership and your organization. The success of the Altus Concept culture shift was due to the enlisted force leading the transformation collectively. After we implemented the change leadership strategy and started the change process, the enlisted force drove the momentum of the new leadership culture and mindset.

Although the initial vision for the Altus Concept was the council's vision, it soon became the entire enlisted force vision. They took ownership for the leadership development program and their leadership development. The key to success for the organizational culture change was a top down process that engaged the entire organization. Integrating the new culture and mindset into the day-to-day operation of the business helped to produce the culture shift we were trying to achieve.

The learning culture established at Altus Air Force Base energized all enlisted personnel to continuously learn, grow and develop themselves. We worked to tear down group and squadron boundaries and make learning and sharing of information an integral part of the daily culture.

Notes

_____

_____

_____

_____

_____

_____

_____

_____

_____

Key Takeaways

Ensure leadership behavior and organizational culture is aligned

The words and actions of organizational leaders must be congruent to the organizational culture. A leader must walk the walk, not just talk the talk.

Reinforce organizational core values

Core values are an important part of organizational culture. An organizational leader must lead by example and reinforce the organizational core values.

Use visual displays to reinforce the culture shift

Use posters, websites, social media and other ways to visually remind and visually reinforce the cultural changes.

Leadership Application

The following are 7 strategies for changing the culture of your organization:

- Develop a people-focused vision and talent development strategy
- Set high standards, hold others responsible and accountable for their development
- Develop a clear set of competencies for your leadership development
- Develop a clear set of characteristics for your leadership development
- Use a multidisciplinary approach to developing leaders
- Have good mentors and leadership coaches for leadership development
- Have your senior leaders be teachers, mentors and role models and live authentically

Leadership Thought Questions

- How effective is the culture in your organization?

- How do you as a leader manage cultural change?

- How does your organization manage cultural change?

- How is your organization investing in a leadership culture?

- What key themes and messages do you use to signify the culture shift?

F(X) Insight

- **Culture management is a leadership challenge**

- **Be sure you are prepared to lead through major changes**

- **Develop solid change management plans**

- **Keep your people informed of the change**

- **Reinforce the change management plan**

- **Identify your culture shift with key themes and messages**

Culture Exercise

The purpose of this writing exercise is to review your current organizational culture and assess its effectiveness. On a separate piece of paper, or on the lines below describe your culture and how it is implemented and if it has organization wide buy-in. What changes in your culture would you like to see? How can you make the changes? What will you do with this new information to help your organization?

Notes

_____

_____

_____

_____

_____

_____

_____

_____

_____

_____

F(X) Leadership Growth and Development Plan

After reading this chapter, review and reflect on the ideas and concepts presented. Think about how to integrate the ideas or concepts into one of the three growth and development areas--Personal, Professional or Leadership Competency. Think about what opportunities, challenges, resources or blind spots you may encounter when you begin your growth and development journey. Use the following questions to help you grow and develop.

1. What area will the ideas and concepts help me grow and develop?

    - Personal

    - Professional

    - Leadership

2. How will I incorporate this new talent or skill into my development?

3. What is my timeline for learning the new talent or skill?

4. What opportunity and resources exist for me to use this new talent or skill?

    - _____

    - _____

    - _____

5. What blind spots may derail me from using this new talent or skill?

    - _____

    - _____

    - _____

Chapter 13

Building our Replacements

> **Key Leadership Concept**: Authentic leaders develop their replacements and look for talent, skills and potential in their people. This is important because each person has different goals, ideas, skills and leadership potential. A leader must be flexible and adaptive to quickly respond to crisis and to change. A leader maintains mission effectiveness during major changes in work tasks or work environment. An authentic leader serves their people by rising above their own self-interests and embraces personal sacrifice and risk for the good of the organization and mission.

MSgt Larry Williams was the Superintendent, Airlift Student Flight, 97th Training Squadron at Altus Air Force Base when I arrived in June 2004. He was in charge of a team of military training leaders and provided mentorship and Airmanship training for 300 new Airmen annually reporting for aircrew duty. MSgt Williams was a leader that understood learning is the path to self-development but also leadership.

An F(X) Principled Leader

In 2004, he completed three Community College of the Air Force associate degrees in applied science - aircrew operations, instructor of military science and maintenance technology, and in 2005 he completed a Bachelor of Science degree in professional aeronautics.

MSgt Williams was a key leader and instructor in the Airmen's Time program and helped to create curriculum and courseware. He used his background and experience as an instructor to mentor, coach and teach new aircrew how to be Airmen and he used this same talent to develop leaders in the Airmen's Time program. He had a passion for taking raw talent and forging them into leaders and he did this in his squadron and throughout the wing.

In 2006, MSgt Williams was promoted to Senior Master Sergeant and selected to attend the Navy Senior Enlisted Academy for Professional Military Education. This Joint development is a critical part of his growth and development as a leader and expanded his understanding of the Navy, as well as the Joint environment. In 2008, MSgt Williams completed a master's degree in business and in 2009 he was promoted to Chief Master Sergeant.

Why is Chief Master Sergeant Larry Williams's story important? After serving as a Command Chief Master Sergeant, he voluntarily returned to be a squadron superintendent to start teaching the next generation of Airmen the leadership principles he learned at Altus. He is an example of a leader who understands the F(X) principles of continuous growth and continuous development to increase his and his organization's leadership capability and capacity.

Developing Warrior Leaders

The first developmental process to start was the integration of pre-deployment training, called Battlefield Deployment Training (BDT), in August 2004. It provided multi-functional contingency and warfighting skills training for Altus Air Force Base deploying forces, with the expressed goal of improving the ability to lead in a VUCA environment, both individually and as part of a joint team. This training emphasized individual and team leading skills to respond and react in a simulated deployed environment and simulated crisis.

Since this was the first training to be implemented before we executed the strategic communications plan, wing personnel met it with resistance. Top-down leadership support at all levels (Wing Commander, Vice Wing Commander, Group Commanders and Chiefs) was crucial to the implementation and integration of the pre-deployment training and the enlisted development courses on the installation. After the implementation of the strategic communications plan and the top-down support, the cultural changes started to take hold.

The BDT trained Altus Air Force Base expeditionary combat warriors prior to deployment. The Superintendent, 97th Mission Support Group, oversaw a 14-member highly experienced cadre that collectively executed BDT. Training focused on five basic areas: Survive, See, Shoot, Move and Communicate. This training provided, for many personnel, their only opportunity to learn and practice skills needed to survive and operate in a VUCA battle space. This training required us to look at ways to improve training and make it more realistic through simulations and "what if" exercises. Altus BDT training created an environment where two objectives were met. The first objective was the five training areas below:

- Individual/Team Movement Leadership
- Weapons Knowledge/Utilization
- Convoy Operations
- Close Quarters Operations and Crisis Thinking
- Military Operations in Urban Terrain

The second objective was an Airman mindset adjustment:

- Leadership is never an option (be aggressive)
- Intelligence drives operations -- operations drive training (train to task)
- The harder right versus the easier wrong -- Core Values Always
- Followership is as important as leadership (own the orders from above)
- Train like you fight -- no slack! (Good enough-- isn't)
- Every Airman a Warrior -- FIRST!

BDT forced the individuals to think and rely on each other as team members and to think critically under pressure. The scenarios were adaptive so that each time it was different. This forced the team to constantly think of options versus getting too comfortable with a predictable outcome. It forced the teams to think non-linear and prepared them for uncertainty. It also pushed them to rely on their training and to adapt it to the environment.

The results and exit surveys helped to establish the necessary senior leadership buy-in for the next part of Airmen's Time Professional and Leadership Development and illustrated the desired end-state for training our expeditionary combat warriors. It established the method of training personnel needed to deploy and their unit's responsibilities to provide that training to meet the needs of the Air Force.

We continued to refine the structure of the deployment training and teambuilding exercises to provide flexible and adaptive individuals. The concept required absolute buy-in at all levels, from the shop supervisors to the senior leadership. After the success of the first developmental project, we turned to enlisted professional and leadership development.

Developing Future Leaders

The second developmental process integrated enlisted professional and leadership development in December 2004. The first leadership challenge for the enlisted professional development process was how to train 1,367 enlisted personnel every month. A training infrastructure and organizational leadership development strategy was developed before the first class could be taught.

The training infrastructure needed to fit a one-hour lesson plan and accommodate 1,367 enlisted personnel every month without affecting the daily mission. This was not an easy task and took two months to develop; however, the Senior Master Sergeants prevailed and our leadership development started in December 2004.

After the infrastructure was in place, the Senior Master Sergeants utilized the Air Force Non-Commissioned Officer Enhancement courses as our first curriculum for training. Our first class taught was *The Enlisted Force Structure* (AFI 36-2618) in which we trained 942 Airmen in the first month. Each month an exit survey for each class was utilized to determine the effectiveness of the lessons taught and the effectiveness of each facilitator.

The survey was a Likert style survey with a rating scale of one for lowest and four for highest. The following criteria was utilized:

1 = The objective of this lesson was met
2 = Lesson content was adequate
3 = Length of lesson was adequate
4 = Visual aids were conducive to learning
5 = Facilitator demonstrated thorough knowledge of subject
6 = This lesson will assist me in meeting my responsibilities as outlined in AFI 36-2618

In August 2005, we expanded our professional development into leadership development realm. The Senior Non-Commissioned Officers started the John Maxwell leadership series, *21 Irrefutable Laws of Leadership,* as part of their leadership development, the Non-Commissioned Officers worked on Teambuilding and the Airmen started a Leadership and Followership course.

Further leadership courseware was developed for our Non-Commissioned Officers and Airmen. It was developed from the U.S. Marine Corps Corporals Course by a core of Senior Non-Commissioned Officers and Non-Commissioned Officers who dedicated themselves to developing more courses tailored to pace our career progression as outlined in AFI 36-2618. In addition, a *Leadership at Gettysburg* course and the John Maxwell course, *The 360 Leader,* was taught later in the development of the program.

Topics such as managing diversity, understanding the effect of sexual harassment on mission effectiveness, leadership development, understanding core competencies, manpower management, conflict management, strategic thinking and progressive discipline were developed.

Learning activities included designated readings from the Chief of Staff of the Air Force, guided discussions of those readings, case studies or "what ifs" simulations and scenarios.

The "what if "simulations or scenarios were guided discussions and table top exercises of "what if" this happens in the future, how do we prepare for it as an organization? Do we have the right learning tactics, techniques, and procedures? Do we have the right leadership bench? This helped develop further classes and curriculum.

Strategic Partnership

In November 2005, we formed a strategic partnership with Air War College to assist us with our leadership development. Colonel Scott Johnson, Chairman, Department of Leadership & Ethics, provided five wing-wide Force Development and Leadership Seminars targeted at:

- Senior Leadership
- Civilians
- Officers and Senior Non-Commissioned Officers
- Squadron Commanders and First Sergeants
- Non-Commissioned Officers and Airmen

Over 600 wing personnel attended these targeted seminars and reinforced the development that we started in December 2004. These seminars helped guide our future development of enlisted professional development, officer professional development and civilian development.

An unintended return of investment of Airmen's Time was the wing's focus on total force professional development transformation of the enlisted, officer and civilian work forces. The professional development programs for the officers and the civilians were based on the enlisted program.

The wing leadership process targeted leadership and professional development in four levels. The Altus Concept 2006 focused on developing Senior Wing Leadership while continuing to develop our Team and Organizational Stakeholders (Lt Col through Lt, Senior Master Sergeant through Airman Basic and Civilian employees). By utilizing this multi-layered approach, we can continue the growth and development of all our leaders across the wing.

Return on Investment

The return on investment for the Altus concept project was found in the innovation and culture change.

- **Bond Airman to the Air Force Core Values**
  Integrity First, Service before Self, and Excellence In All We Do. A Back to the Basics approach and the development of the STRIPES poster was a great modeling tool that helped to reinforce that bond for our Airmen. It drove home the importance and the sacrifice that is required to wear the Air Force Enlisted Chevrons.

- **Build Skills Competence**
  Building competent and skilled warriors was our main idea. Altus was #1 of 13 AETC bases for maintaining the lowest number of personnel in excessive training and #2 regarding CDC pass rate of 96.2 percent with 65 Airmen scoring 90 percent or better.

- **Build Expeditionary Expertise**
  Our battlefield deployment course equipped our deploying warriors for the rigors of combat under the concept "Sweat more in peace, bleed less in War". It was our overall objective to prepare our warriors for the fight and to bring them home again.

- **Build Expertise Through Mentoring**
  We mentored, taught and reinforced Air Force heritage through "12 0'clock High Stories", enlisted calls, first sergeant panels, SNCO panels, Chiefs' panels, Commanders panels and leadership seminars.

- **Build Air Force Cultural Awareness**
  We conducted numerous Enlisted Heritage projects from past Senior Enlisted Advisor Luncheons to our current project called "What it means to wear these Stripes".

- **Build Joint and Coalition Knowledge**
  Our joint partnership with Command Sergeant Major William High and the Ft. Sill schoolhouse helped to increased our warrior leadership training, while our interagency partnership with Defense Information Systems Agency (DISA) increased our Joint and interagency understanding. We developed the Joint STRIPES poster for DISA and it helped our personnel to understand and work with the whole of government team.

Summary

Why is this deliberate process of growing and developing leaders important? Developing leaders in an organization is a business necessity; however, it is the lifeblood of a military organization. The military takes men and women right out of high school and college to grow and develop them to be the next generation of leaders. We are constantly building leaders to replace leaders who are leaving. We must set them up for success.

Bottom line: Today, it is no longer enough for leaders or organizations to say, "People are our greatest asset." They need to back it up through a clearly articulated philosophy and by investing in talent development, talent retention and succession planning.

Notes

_____

_____

_____

_____

_____

_____

Key Takeaways

Create a learning environment in which everyone can capitalize on their talents and develop their leadership

Encourage people to expand their horizons to continuously grow, continuously develop and continuously reinvent themselves.

Use coaching, mentoring and teaching skills to develop and grow your people and organization

Teach, coach and mentor by clarifying ideas, explaining principles and standards and by being a role model.

Set performance standards and hold people responsible and accountable for achieving them

Establish clear standards for performance and reward those who achieve excellence.

Leadership Application

The following are 10 strategies for developing leaders:

- Use a deliberate approach to leadership development
- Decide on clear developmental goals
- Challenge and stretch your people's leadership ability and potential through assignments
- Train, educate and develop everyone in the organization
- Set specific leadership development expectations and goals
- Identify performance measures for evaluating personal growth
- Collaboratively establish leadership development plans with each person
- Meet with your people regularly to discuss their progress on developmental goals
- Provide direction and guidance to assist and support the growth and development of your people
- Provide leadership opportunities for your people to use the new skills they have acquired

Leadership Thought Questions

- Does your organization prepare leaders to lead in a VUCA environment?

- How do you measure the success of your leadership and professional development programs?

- What strategic alliances does your organization have to build your leaders?

- Are you investing time now to develop a leadership bench for the future?

- Is your organization a continuous learning environment?

- Have you set clear expectations for your people to grow and develop?

- Do you have a disciplined approach to development or is it haphazard?

F(X) Insight

- **Take the time to invest in your organization and build your future leaders**

- **Leadership development is an organization necessity**

- **Develop your leadership pipeline and seek out your high-potential leaders**

- **Look for your late blooming leaders**

- **Build strategic alliances to further your development process**

- **Reinforce your organizational core values**

Strategic Planning Exercise

The purpose of this writing exercise is to review your current organizational leadership development plan and assess its effectiveness. On a separate piece of paper, or on the lines below, write down what key skills, talents, and mindsets your team or your organization will need to meet future challenges and opportunities. After you define, the leadership requirements, assess how well your organization is currently developing the talents, skills and mindsets for the future. What will you do with this new information to help your organization?

Notes

_____

_____

_____

_____

_____

_____

_____

_____

_____

_____

_____

F(X) Leadership Growth and Development Plan

After reading this chapter, review and reflect on the ideas and concepts presented. Think about how to integrate the ideas or concepts into one of the three growth and development areas--Personal, Professional or Leadership Competency. Think about what opportunities, challenges, resources or blind spots you may encounter when you begin your growth and development journey. Use the following questions to help you grow and develop.

1.   What area will the ideas and concepts help me grow and develop?

    • Personal

    • Professional

    • Leadership

2.   How will I incorporate this new talent or skill into my development?

3.   What is my timeline for learning the new talent or skill?

4.   What opportunity and resources exist for me to use this new talent or skill?

    • _____

    • _____

    • _____

5.   What blind spots may derail me from using this new talent or skill?

    • _____

    • _____

    • _____

Chapter 14

Results Driven Leadership

> **Key Leadership Concept**: Leadership is fundamental to all military units. Forging future military leaders is the responsibility of current leaders. Persistent professional and leadership development is the tool to do so. Developing those leaders in a deliberate process guarantees the military has the right people, in the right place and at the right time. Leadership and professional development must continue to provide the military with its most valuable resource: its people, its motivated and qualified personnel.

In February 2006, Colonel Johnson, Chairman, Department of Leadership and Ethics, conducted a 360-degree leadership mirror survey on the Altus Air Force Base leadership--Commander, Vice Commander, Command Chief, Group Commanders, Squadron Commanders, Chief Master Sergeants, Senior Master Sergeants and First Sergeants.

Leadership-Based Outcomes

A 360-degree feedback is a systematic method of amassing views and opinions about an individual's performance from an extensive array of coworkers. This could include peers, subordinates and the boss, along with people outside the organization, such as customers.

A total of 40 leadership personnel took part in the survey. The survey instructions asked each leader to send the survey to their boss, peers, subordinates and other personnel they might influence in their leadership role.

The results of the leadership mirror survey were briefed to the leadership in April 2006. The survey indicated the overall opinion of wing leadership was very high with the highest rated items by rater group in the areas of leading by example (links his/her responsibilities with the mission of the whole organization), change management (in implementing a change, explains, answers questions and patiently listens to concerns), innovation (promotes a culture of innovation and creative thinking), internal and external communication (promotes and encourages and open flow of communication) and talent development (develops employees by providing challenge and opportunity).

The overall raw comments from the survey indicated a positive image of base leadership due to the dedicated commitment of investing time and money to leadership, battlefield and career development.

Combining the 360-Degree Leadership Mirror feedback, the results of the 2006 Wing Climate Assessment and the results from the 2006 Air Education and Training Command Inspector General Inspection report, Airmen's Time exceeded its goals.

It built a culture of innovation, teamwork and growth that spread throughout the wing and developed leaders for the future. After I left Altus Air Force Base, I kept track of the 40 original enlisted team members that helped develop and who taught as instructors. The original make-up of the 40-team members was:

- 10 Senior Master Sergeants - EFDC
- 10 Master Sergeants - Instructors
- 10 Technical Sergeants - Instructors
- 10 Staff Sergeants - Instructors

Promotions

Nineteen of the original 40 team members were promoted or are currently serving as Chief Master Sergeants/Senior Master Sergeants, which is a 48 percent promotion rate.

- 9 of the 10 Senior Master Sergeants -- promoted to Chief Master Sergeant
- 10 of the 20 Master Sergeants/Technical Sergeants -- promoted to Senior Master Sergeant/Chief Master Sergeant
- 2 of the original Staff Sergeants -- STEP promoted to Technical Sergeants and are now Master Sergeants

Career Choices

Of the original 20 Master Sergeants/Technical Sergeants

- 5 became First Sergeants

- 4 became Airmen Leadership School Flight Chiefs
- One served as a Command Chief

Side Note: The Wing Commanders and Group Commanders who enabled and backed the program also had successful careers.

- Colonel Solo was promoted to Major General and served as the last 19th Air Force Commander
- Colonel Everhart is currently a Major General and is still serving today
- Colonel Dillon is a Major General and is still serving today
- Colonel Medler is a Brigadier General and is still serving today

Data Collection

The benefit of collecting data of this kind is that it solidified the original intent and vision behind Airmen's Time. The overarching principle in our concept was that leadership resides in everyone. Leadership in this concept is not necessarily associated with rank and position, but is fundamentally associated with qualities, such as drive, vision, innovation, creativity and passion.

Airmen's Time produced a new focus on total force professional and leadership development of the officer and civilian work force resulting in a consolidated Warrior Professional Development Center. The leadership philosophy change produced outcomes that validated the Airmen's Time development process. It changed from an individual leadership development focus to a collective leadership development focus

The program produced the outcomes the EFDC wanted and the results subsequently validated by an outside agency focused on compliance and standards.

Airmen's Time produced a synergistic outcome during the 2006 Operational Readiness Inspection—resulting in "Outstanding" ratings in Force Development, Standards, Career Assistance Advisor and First Term Airmen Center programs.

The Altus Leadership and Force Development Website evolved from a Career Assistance Advisor website into a powerful professional development knowledge center and feedback tool utilized and visited by 12,872 visitors ranging from US Army, Air National Guard, Headquarters Air Force and 50 other Air Force Bases.

The website also spawned two other Leadership and Force Development websites in Yokota Air Base and Ali Al Salem Air Base. The Strategic Leadership team established collaborative partnerships with Vance and Little Rock Air Force Base to share professional development ideas and lessons. The original Air Force "My EDP" website was built in accordance with "Airmen's Time" concepts and enlisted flight plans.

Comments

Air Force leaders who saw the process commented the following:

- The Commander and Command Chief of Air Education and Training Command called the program, "Outstanding!"

- 5th Chief Master Sergeant of the Air Force, Bob Gaylor, lauded program as "Synergistic"

- Chief Master Sergeant of the Air Force, Gerald Murray, "If you want to do leadership development right go to Altus"

- 19th Air Force Command Chief called the program, "Phenomenal"

- Director of Ethics and Leadership at Air War College said, "program is an Air Force benchmark"

- Director, College of Enlisted Professional Military Education cited the program as, "Awesome program...Great leadership"

- Airmen's Time requested by AF/A1PFE during Leadership and Force Development conference

Beyond Altus

In May 2006, the Defense Information Systems Agency Command Senior Enlisted established a Joint Enlisted Force Development Council (JEFDC) based on the Altus EFDC Charter and used Airmen's Time: The Altus Concept to establish a Joint Enlisted Professional Development Process for the Agency. During the collaborative workshop, the Joint S.T.R.I.P.E.S. poster was developed and adopted for the program.

In January 2009, when I became the USSTRATCOM Command Senior Enlisted Leader the Joint S.T.R.I.P.E.S. poster and the Joint EFDC charter was adopted and implemented to establish the USSTRATCOM

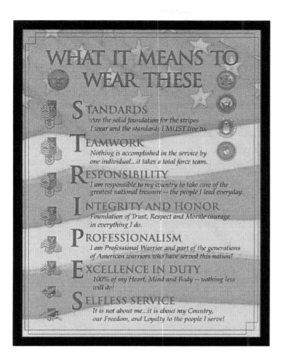

JEFDC. It was also the basis for "The Year of the Enlisted Global Warfighter" program and the basis for the USSTRATCOM Enlisted University program. Both of these programs focused on the enlisted professional and leadership development.

Summary

In the end, Airmen's Time: The Altus Concept, was a highly successful journey. It developed a strong culture based on our core values, teamwork, diversity, respect leadership development, and transformational change, It developed a strong outcomes-focused performance culture within the EFDC and the Enlisted Corps. Airmen's Time fostered a leadership culture that crossed group boundaries and established a strong team culture.

Several concepts of Airmen's Time were eventually adopted as part of the Air Force culture. Airmen's Time Training was inculcated into Basic Military Training and Technical Training as part of the daily interaction for Military Training Instructors to discuss what they did that day and to help new recruits and Airmen adjust to the Air Force.

Many of the Altus Concepts were adopted as part of the Air Force culture, too. The developmental flight plans developed at Altus Air Force Base were the first developmental flight plans for My Enlisted Development Plan (My EDP). The Altus Enlisted Force Development Council and its charter were the precursor to stand up the Air Force level Enlisted Force Development Council in 2008.

Finally, it created a culture of achievement and collaboration when it expanded into programs for the Air Force, a Defense Combat Support Agency and a Combatant Command.

Key Takeaways

Measure and assess the results of your development plan/project

A good way to measure how your program is working is a return on investment review. We used the 360-degree mirror, climate assessment, Likert surveys, promotions and outside agencies as our method of review to make our program better and to provide a better program to develop our people.

Invite other people and agencies to assess your program

Your program is about developing people and increasing the effectiveness of your organization, not about how well you are as a leader. Inviting outside agencies or leaders to review and assess your program ensures you have not created a self-licking ice cream cone.

Leadership Application

The following are 10 strategies for a successful leadership program:

- Envision the vision before you start and develop a strategy to accomplish the vision
- Know your people and your organization well enough to identify leadership gaps and challenges
- Get senior leadership on board early and keep them informed and involved
- Identify your key movers and shakers and get them excited an inspired
- Build a team that understands the vision and can accomplish it
- Fight for development funds and show a return on investment
- Start your communication plan early
- Respond to employee apathy quickly
- Recognize and reward your key leaders' performance
- Have another set of eyes review your program

F(X) Insight

- Invest in your people and reap the rewards
- Your people are not just employees, they are valuable assets to the growth of your organization
- Expect results
- Innovation and creativity are a result of developing and investing in people
- Always use the Golden Rule: Treat Others as you yourself want to be treated.

Notes

_____

_____

_____

_____

_____

_____

_____

_____

_____

F(X) Leadership Growth and Development Plan

After reading this chapter, review and reflect on the ideas and concepts presented. Think about how to integrate the ideas or concepts into one of the three growth and development areas--Personal, Professional or Leadership Competency. Think about what opportunities, challenges, resources or blind spots you may encounter when you begin your growth and development journey. Use the following questions to help you grow and develop.

1. What area will the ideas and concepts help me grow and develop?

   - Personal

   - Professional

   - Leadership

2. How will I incorporate this new talent or skill into my development?

3. What is my timeline for learning the new talent or skill?

4. What opportunity and resources exist for me to use this new talent or skill?

   - _____

   - _____

   - _____

5. What blind spots may derail me from using this new talent or skill?

   - _____

   - _____

   - _____

Conclusion

One of my favorite self-development/leadership development movies is *A Knight's Tale* with Heath Ledger. The story is about personal change, self-awareness, crisis management, success, failure, leadership experience, growth and development in the three competence areas...Personal, Professional and Leadership. It is also about a disciplined approach to development, taking responsibility for your life and continuously reinventing yourself as you grow and develop.

A poignant part of the movie shows how young William gets his start in which you see a father taking his son to be a knight's page. His father wanted his son to have a different life than a thatcher, so he lets his son become a page for a Knight. His father was his first mentor and he taught him the craft of roof thatching.

Thatching was hard work, and by learning this craft, he developed discipline and an attitude of service. If he stayed, he would only be a thatcher, nothing more nothing less. As they part his father says, "this is all I can do for you...watch and learn...go and change your stars." This is the first trial for the young leader. He is leaving his first mentor and now is under the tutelage of Sir Ector, his new mentor. He quickly learns self-reliance, how to follow and how to be a member of a team.

The next three big life lessons for the leader are decision-making, risk taking and courage. In the movie, the old knight dies just before he is about to win the tournament. The young leader, who has gone from being a page to a squire, has grown up in the mentoring of the Knight and his team, takes a risk and decides he will enter the tournament and fight.

He steps up as a leader to take care of his team in order for all of them to survive. His courage to face the overwhelming challenge changes the fate of him and that of the team. The win inspires him and gives him confidence he did not have prior to the challenge. From this newfound confidence is his ability, he decides to become a Knight. His teammates realize he is not ready and he needs more training and development to meet the challenges of the VUCA environment.

After a period of training and development, the team heads to their first tournament, and along the way they realize they cannot fight under the old knight's name and must invent a new name and leadership persona. This is the first time we see the young leader reinvent himself.

He is no longer William; he is a Knight. He has begun the change process. As he competes in tournaments, he gains the professional experience he needs to be a Knight, he gains confidence and self-awareness in his personal life, and as he becomes a Knight, he gains wisdom in his leadership as a team leader.

Part of this change process is the issue of the old armor and new armor. The old armor of the old Knight is the leadership style and teachings of the status quo. As William develops and grows as a leader, his style and his tactics develop, he breaks out of the shell of his old mentor and becomes his own leader.

He puts on the armor of his new leadership, which helps him meet the challenges of the VUCA environment he is encountering. The new armor is light, mobile and allows him greater range of movement against his competitors. He is light, lean and lethal. He has reinvented himself again. The student has surpassed his two mentors.

As he continues to meet the challenges of the tournaments, he grows from thinking that he is a Knight to becoming a Knight. He has emerged from being a thatcher's son, a page and a squire, to the top of his profession. He is now the expert. His true leadership emerges when his identity is discovered and he is about to be arrested.

Instead of running from the challenges and adversity, he stands his ground and proclaims that he will not run and that he is a Knight. He accepts what is about to happen to him and accepts the consequences for his decisions. Through his trials, development and experiences he has become the leader he envisioned himself to be. There is no turning back for him...he chose to "Inspire and not Retire". He is a Knight in the oldest tradition--chivalrous, noble and authentic.

The Prince of England knights him because he recognizes his true leadership, his true purpose and his ability to inspire. Sir William has completed the transformation of his life. Through his disciplined approach and desire to become better, he became victorious in life, his career and leadership. In the end, he "changed his stars".

What is your leadership story?

In the beginning of the book I stated that leadership principles are timeless, unfortunately, we are not. We have a finite time here to make a difference and to leave some sort of legacy. If you knew how much time you had to spend on earth would you make different decisions? Would you stop wasting time? Would you take yourself more serious?

F(X) Leadership is about the difference you make in yourself and in your people's lives every day. It is about the effects and outcomes you want for your life. It is about taking responsibility for your growth and development. F(X) leadership is not about power, position or personality, it is about authenticity, service and preparing yourself for the challenges of life. It is being serious with your approach to developing yourself to be ready for whatever life throws at you. F(X) leadership is not giving in or giving up on yourself. The time is now to radically change your life, career and leadership.

Discover your purpose and then passionately pursue it

The first thing you need to do as a leader is to awaken the leader within you. It is about discovering your true self. It is about seizing control of your life by discovering your purpose, envisioning your future and writing your personal vision and mission statement. It is about not wasting your time.

Truly effective leaders are those who have figured out what is important to them, what matters in their life and what they stand for. They have identified their purpose and are living it daily. F(X) leaders passionately pursue their purpose in life and relentlessly challenge themselves to become better. Few things are more important to a leader than a vision for their life and a mission statement to achieve that vision.

Be transformed by the renewing of your heart, mind, body and soul

Everyday look for ways to renew yourself and build resiliency into your life. Go to the gym or for a walk to strengthen your body. Read a book or take a class to keep your mind focused and thoughtful. Go to your favorite place to worship to renew your soul. Seek out God. Spend time with family and friends to fortify the love in your heart. Finally, energy and enthusiasm are two of the necessary qualities a leader needs to survive and thrive. By renewing yourself you stay energetic and enthusiastic.

Forget the past and move toward the future

Learn from your past mistakes and your past successes, but don't try to relive them. Progress is about moving forward in your life, career and leadership. Holding on to the past will hold you back from future achievements. By forgetting what is behind you and driving toward the future you will continue to grow, develop and reinvent yourself.

Teach Others

Take time to teach others how to find their purpose and share a piece of your life with them. The best way to learn something is to teach it to another person. It is also the best way to let other people know that you care about their development and are interested in their growth.

Encouragement and Grace

A leader is an agent of hope. Your people want to become the very best they can be and through your leadership they will. Provide encouragement as they grow and develop, it will lift them up and provide the confidence to continue. Bestow grace when they make mistakes. It is very easy to yell and get angry over mistakes, but by doing so you miss an opportunity to continue to develop the person. Show them the error of their ways but reinforce the correct way to do the task or job.

Be a Servant Leader

I believe we are hard-wired to connect and serve with one another. If we were not hard-wired to connect then social media would not have lasted as long as it has. We need to communicate and connect with one another. Serving one another is an outcropping of our leadership and how we develop others.

Inspire or Retire

Finally, Inspire or Retire. The Motto **"Inspire or Retire"** is a reminder to always inspire yourself and your people. As a leader, if you can no longer inspire your people it is time to step aside and let someone else take the lead. People are looking for leaders who inspire them. They are looking for meaning and purpose, not trophies and awards. When authentic leaders inspire people, they reach new levels of innovation, achievement and commitment.

Lead Fearlessly

When General John Reynolds was killed in the first day's fighting at Gettysburg, Major General Winfield Scott Hancock took charge on the battlefield. He recommended to General George Meade that the Union Army continue the fight at Gettysburg. He selected the ground on which the army deployed to fight for the second and third day.

Major General Hancock knew that his presence on the battlefield would encourage and embolden his soldiers to stand fast and fight because he was with them through the thick of the fighting. Hancock directed the action in the Union center until wounded. General Hancock led from the front with courageous leadership and by doing so inspired his troops to greatness during Pickett's Charge on the third day of the Gettysburg Battle.

Today's people are looking for the same kind of courageous leadership from their leaders. They need to see courageous leadership from you. They need to see you lead from the front and to inspire them daily toward mission accomplishment. They need you to take a stand on what is right or wrong. They need you to set the example and be the example of Authentic Leadership. Courageous leadership is setting and living the standards daily and being an authentic role model example for them.

Courageous leadership is living your core values and following them daily. Courageous leadership is about integrity. Integrity is the cornerstone of all leadership actions, for without it there is no trust in the leader, no confidence in their actions and their words have no meaning. A courageous leader has to have the ability to make tough decisions and the ability to expect others to make tough decisions. It takes courage to decide to do what is right and not necessarily, what feels good and what fun is at the time.

Be a courageous leader and inspire your people!!!

Final thought

Don't sell yourself short, you only get one chance to make a difference and an impact. Take the time and envision where you want to be 5,10 and 20 years from now then put your plan in to action and achieve your dream!

INSPIRE or RETIRE!

F(X) Chapter Review

Chapter Review

Awaken the Leader Within

> **Key Leadership Concept**: Leadership begins inside of you. Leadership is about you, the people you influence and a belief that you can make a difference and have an impact. Leadership starts with a condition of the heart – the desire and passion to make a difference before it moves to the brain to implement a plan to make a difference. It is an inside-out process and is shaped by your values, character, choices, opportunities, experiences and your worldview.

Key Takeaways

Dedicate yourself to finding your purpose

Your purpose provides you context and focus for your life.

Your purpose defines who you are

Discover your purpose and live a fulfilling life.

Your life purpose makes you unique

Living with purpose means, your life and leadership are congruent.

Chapter Review

The F(X) Leadership Framework

Key Leadership Concept: The F(X) Leadership Model is a proactive, disciplined approach to improving yourself and your leadership. It is the Science behind the Art. We cannot control every aspect of our lives; we can, however, prepare ourselves to be flexible and adaptive in how we react to our unexpected life and leadership challenges. Since I cannot control an environment that is volatile, uncertain, complex and ambiguous, I can prepare myself for the uncertainty through a disciplined approach.

Key Takeaways

Dedicate yourself to a disciplined approach to life

You cannot control every aspect of your life; however, you can prepare yourself through a disciplined approach to your leadership and your life.

Being successful requires hard work and P4R

Become the master artisan, performer or leader you want to be – develop and grow yourself.

Leadership is an art and a science

If you want to be an effective leader, know both parts of leadership.

Chapter Review

Learning is Leading!

> **Key Leadership Concept**: A commitment to a lifelong process of learning is the key to successful leadership. In today's volatile, uncertain, complex and ambiguous environment, learning is vital to your ability to adapt to ever-evolving challenges and uncertainty. Continuous learning, continuous development and continuous growth create the self-awareness for a leader to continually reinvent their capability as a leader and a person.

Key Takeaways

Dedicate yourself to lifelong learning

Self-leadership is the key to leading yourself well and then leading others. Be the leader you want to be by developing yourself first.

Read, read and read some more

Reading is a valuable leadership skill to developing yourself. Reading provides new ideas, concepts and opens your mind to further learning. Read biographies of leaders, read leadership books and read books about your profession.

Continue to develop your character

Character development is vital to leadership. Our character is the true essence of who we are as a person and how we lead as a leader. It is the very core of what drives us and influences our actions and reactions. Character defines our authentic leadership.

Chapter Review

Leadership C2

> **Key Leadership Concept**: Characteristics are leadership attributes, qualities or unique aptitudes and leadership competencies are behaviors, skills or talents for a specific profession or responsibility. In order to develop your leadership growth and development plan you need to identify the leadership characteristics and competencies that will improve your capability and prepare you for future challenges. Your developmental plan should incorporate skills training, leadership experiences, growth opportunities and leadership knowledge development.

Key Takeaways

The world has changed

Developing yourself and your people will ensure you can survive and thrive in the future leadership realm.

Understand the global strategic picture

Look holistically at the changing world leadership environment. Understand the complexity and uncertainty so you can lead through challenges and opportunities.

Characteristics and Competencies are valuable

As a leader, you need to continually add capabilities and abilities to your leadership fitness. Characteristics and competencies provide you a plan for development.

Chapter Review

Developing Your Plan

> **Key Leadership Concept**:. The biggest challenge to a leadership growth and development plan is where do I start? You start by developing a yearly developmental plan and grow it into a long term life plan. A yearly plan allows you to express your vision for the next year, to define your specific goals and objectives and to commit yourself to continuous development and continuous growth actions.

Key Takeaways

You must be a catalyst for change

Growing and developing yourself begins from an inward desire to change. You must be your own change agent.

Purposeful development is the key to continuous growth

Growth and development are not a one-time event, they are continuous and deliberate.

Determine your outcome and effects

Take the initiative and determine your leadership and life needs, then implement your strategy.

Chapter Review

Inspire or Retire!

> **Key Leadership Concept**: Inspire your people, your team and your organization to great heights of professional growth and mission accomplishment or retire so another leader can inspire them. An inspirational leader inspires people to greatness through positive influence and encouragement. Inspired people reach greater heights of performance, creativity and innovation in an organization.

Key Takeaways

Be an inspirational leader

Inspirational leaders empower and unleash their people's creativity, innovation and collaboration.

No bystanders allowed

Be an engaged leader and understand your people and your organization. Leadership is everyone's business.

INSPIRE or RETIRE!

Chapter Review

Know Your People

Key Leadership Concept: There is no leadership without followers. Leadership requires that you know your people and continue to build the relationship you have with your subordinates or followers.

Key Takeaways

Be a teacher, mentor and coach to your people

Shape expectations and inspire your people by being a teacher, mentor and coach. Develop your people to be leaders.

Understand your people's needs and desires

Know your people well—their needs, desires and capabilities to grow and develop them.

Feedback and Dialogue

A leader needs to continue building the relationships through feedback and dialogue to reinforce trust and respect to enlarge and empower their people and team.

Investing in other people is a key aspect of the F(X) Leadership Model. Building leaders assists others in their development and allows you to be a servant leader by helping them grow.

Chapter Review

Airmen's Time: The Altus Concept

Key Leadership Concept: Effective leadership begins at the top and permeates throughout the organization at all levels. This is a crucial factor in assuring that leadership is an organization-wide capability. Leaders at every level in an organization must accept the responsibility to lead, take ownership of their part of the mission and develop their people. The impact of successful leadership cascades across all departments in an organization and can affect the morale of each person. Leaders are linked to organizational culture and organizational effectiveness. Leaders who develop their people guarantee organization success.

Key Takeaways

Seek to understand the issues

A leader needs to identify and evaluate information and then use the information to effect decisions, actions and outcomes for the future.

Develop desired outcomes and strategy

Leadership outcomes and developmental strategies must be aligned with the Organization's mission, vision, core values, goals and strategic plan in order to be successful.

Analyze and use foresight

Critically analyze outcomes and strategy to understand the second, third and fourth order of effects of proposed policies or actions.

Chapter Review

Collaborative Teamwork

> **Key Leadership Concept:** A team is capable of accomplishing things that no individual person, no matter how talented and gifted they are, can do alone. The strength of the team is the individual capabilities and abilities forged into one cohesive organization. A well-functioning team is committed to a common purpose and a common vision.

Key Takeaways

Seek to inspire trust and a higher sense of purpose

Trust is essential to leadership. No one wants to follow an untrustworthy leader. Trust means you are true to your word and you are an authentic leader.

Promote positive teamwork

Positive teamwork supports the organization's goals and objectives and fosters behavior directed toward the achievement of theses ends. Teamwork that supports hard work, loyalty, quality consciousness or concern for customer satisfaction are examples of positive norms.

A team accomplishes more than an individual

A team is capable of accomplishing things that no individual person, no matter how talented and gifted they are, can do alone.

Chapter Review

10

Leadership Models

> **Key Leadership Concept**: Leadership and leadership development is critical to military success in peacetime and war. Identifying, developing and preparing future leaders is the ultimate goal of professional military education, professional development and is a key responsibility of every leader.

Key Takeaways

Leadership development is critical to organizational success

Today, organizational leadership is a necessity. Every person in an organization needs to be able to lead through complexity and ambiguity.

Develop a strategic plan for leadership development

Use an organized, disciplined and well-developed approach to developing your people.

Set high standards and high expectations for your leadership development program

Ensure your people understand that leadership development is not an option, it is a business necessity.

Chapter Review

11

Strategic Communications Plan

Key Leadership Concept: The purpose of the Airmen's Time and Airmen Development communications strategy was to inform and engage wing personnel, to include senior leaders and military, civilian and contractor employees, of the scope and intent of the Airmen's Time program and to discuss the objectives.

Key Takeaways

Communication is the key to informing and engaging people

A well-developed communications plan will eliminate ambiguity and uncertainty in change management.

Develop a strategic communications plan

Change management requires a clear and precise communications plan to ensure everyone involved in the change understands the scope and purpose for the change.

Identify your change agents

Organizational change requires champions who will influence and guide the change in each work center.

Communicate, Communicate and Communicate!

Chapter Review

12

Culture Shift

> **Key Leadership Concept**: The impact of successful leadership cascades across all departments in an organization and can affect the morale of each person. Leaders are the linchpin to the organizations' culture and organizational effectiveness. Leaders who develop their people guarantee organizational success.

Key Takeaways

Ensure leadership behavior and organizational culture is aligned

The words and actions of organizational leaders must be congruent to the organizational culture. A leader must walk the walk, not just talk the talk.

Reinforce organizational core values

Core values are an important part of organizational culture. An organizational leader must lead by example and reinforce the organizational core values.

Use visual displays to reinforce the culture shift

Use posters, websites, social media and other ways to visually remind and visually reinforce cultural changes.

Chapter Review

Building our Replacements

Key Leadership Concept: Authentic leaders develop their replacements and look for talent, skills and potential in their people. This is important because each person has different goals, ideas, skills and leadership potential. A leader must be flexible and adaptive to quickly respond to crisis and to change. A leader maintains mission effectiveness during major changes in work tasks or work environment. An authentic leader serves their people by rising above their own self-interests and embraces personal sacrifice and risk for the good of the organization and mission.

Key Takeaways

Create a learning environment in which everyone can capitalize on their talents and develop their leadership

Encourage people to expand their horizons to continuously grow, continuously develop and continuously reinvent themselves.

Use coaching, mentoring and teaching skills to develop and grow your people and organization

Teach, coach and mentor by clarifying ideas, explaining principles and standards and by being a role model.

Set performance standards and hold people responsible and accountable for achieving them

Establish clear standards for performance and reward those who achieve excellence.

Chapter Review

Results Driven Leadership

> **Key Leadership Concept**: Leadership is fundamental to all military units. Forging future military leaders is the responsibility of current leaders. Persistent professional and leadership development is the tool to do so. Developing those leaders in a deliberate process guarantees the military has the right people, in the right place and at the right time. Leadership and professional development must continue to provide the military with its most valuable resource: its people, its motivated and qualified personnel.

Key Takeaways

Measure and assess the results of your development plan/project

A good way to measure how your program is working is a return on investment review. We used the 360-degree mirror, climate assessment, Likert surveys, promotions and outside agencies as our method of review to make our program better and to provide a better program to develop our people.

Invite other people and agencies to assess your program

Your program is about developing people and increasing the effectiveness of your organization, not about how well you are as a leader. Inviting outside agencies or leaders to review and assess your program ensures you have not created a self-licking ice cream cone.

Research and References

Air Force Education Training Command (2008), *On learning the future of Air Force education and training*, Retrieved Mar 22, 2012, from http://www.aetc.af.mil

Air Force Doctrine Directive 1-1, (2006), Retrieved June 9, 2009, from http://www-e-publishing.af.mil/AFDD1-1.

Air Force Instruction 36-2618. (2009). Retrieved Mar 22, 2009 from http://www-e-publishing.af.mil/AFI36-2618.

Air Force Pamphlet 36-2241. (2007). Retrieved Mar 22, 2009 from http://www.e-publishing.af.mil/AFPAM36-2241

Air Force Posture Statement. (2006). Retrieved Mar 22, 2009 from http://www.af.mil/AFPS

Bennis, W. (1989). *On becoming a leader.* Reading, MA: Addison-Wesley Publishing Co

Bethel, S. (2009). *A new breed of leader,* Berkley Books, New York

Burns, J. M. (1978). *Leadership.* NY: Harper & Row.

Challenges of warfare in the 21st century (2009). Retrieved July 18, 2009 from http://www.af.mil/information/speeches

Chappelow, C. 360-degree feedback. In McCauley, C. D. & Van Velsor, E. (2004). *Handbook of leadership development.* (2nd Ed) Jossey-Bass.

Collins, J. (2001). *Good to great.* NY: Harper Collins.

Collins, J. (2003). *Built to last.* NY: Harper Collins.

Covey, S. (2004). *The 8th Habit: from effectiveness to greatness,* Simon & Schuster, Inc, NY

Denhardt, R., Denhardt, J., & Aristigueta, M., (2009). *Managing human behavior in public and nonprofit organizations.* Thousand Oaks CA: Sage Publications

Gardner, H. (2006). *Five minds for the future.* Harvard Business School Press, Boston, Mass.

George, W. (2003). *Authentic leadership: rediscovering the secrets to creating lasting value;* Jossey-Bass, San Francisco

Kouzes, J & Posner, B. (2006). *A leaders legacy,* Jossey-Bass, San Francisco, CA

Kouzes, J & Posner, B. (2003). *The leadership challenge.*(3rd Ed) Jossey-Bass Inc., Publishers.

Maxwell, J. (1998). *21 irrefutable laws of leadership,* Thomas Nelson, Nashville, TN

McCauley, C. & Van Velsor, E. (2004). *Handbook of leadership development* (2nd Ed.) Jossey-Bass Inc, Publishers

Schmitt, J. (2009), *Command and (out of) control: The military implications of complexity theory.* Retrieved Mar 23, 2012 from http://www.ndu.edu

ABOUT THE AUTHOR

Thomas S. Narofsky is the Founder and Chief Inspirational Officer for the Narofsky Consulting Group, a leadership development, team effectiveness, and executive coaching consultancy. He the developer of the F(X) Leadership Model and the Inspire or Retire Leadership Theorem.

Thom retired in November 2011 as the Command Senior Enlisted Leader for United States Strategic Command after serving 28 years on active duty in the United States Air Force. In his capacity as a Combatant Command Senior Enlisted Leader, he served on the Department of Defense Senior Enlisted Leader Council and the United States Strategic Command Joint Enlisted Development Council which focused on all matters concerning joint and combined total force integration, mission readiness, utilization and professional and leadership development of the joint enlisted force. He also served on the United States Air Force Enlisted Board of Directors which focused on professional development, training concepts and long-range strategies to provide continuous, career-long enlisted deliberate development by integrating education, training and experience to produce a skilled and adaptive work force. He has conducted worldwide professional and leadership development seminars with U.S, Korean, Japanese, Australian, British, Canadian, Belgian and German enlisted forces. His military decorations include Defense Superior Service Medal and the Bronze Star.

Thom is an adjunct professor at Bellevue University in the Arts and Sciences Department. He holds a Master of Arts in Leadership, a Master of Science in Information Technology Management and a Bachelor of Science in Interdisciplinary Studies.